THE JOYFUL EDUCATOR

Cultivating an Inspiring Teaching Experience and a Fulfilling Life Outside the Classroom

DR. EDWARD J. SPURKA

Paperback ISBN: # 979-8-9988965-0-7
Electronic ISBN: # 979-8-9988965-1-4

Library of Congress Control Number: # 2025909694

Portions of this book are works of nonfiction. Certain names and identifying characteristics have been changed.

Printed in the United States of America.

Publishing Consultant, PRESStinely: PRESStinely.com

Dr. Edward J. Spurka
SpurkaEdInstitute.com

Contents

INTRODUCTION

In the spring of 2024, I ran into a good friend of mine who I worked with for over 15 years. Carole had retired several years ago and asked me how much longer I had before I retired from education. I glared at her and told her that I was never going to retire. I loved my job, and my energy tank was full! I was in my 33rd year of education. I told her about the joy I was having at work and how I recently led a mission trip to Eswatini, Africa, coached girls' flag football, and focused my energy on celebrating my teachers and students. I went to work every day with a smile on my face, which showed my teachers and students how much I loved being an educator. As an administrator, my teachers would always tell me they wouldn't want my job because of how hard it was. I always told them that they had the most important and hardest job in education and that my job wasn't harder. It was just a 'different' hard.

While I knew my years were adding up, I was never more motivated, and there was never a Monday morning when I wasn't excited to start my week. I must admit that I am human and did appreciate an occasional three-day weekend or a snow day! I told Carole I loved being an educator and would never retire! She responded to me with a gentle smile, "You know, EJS, sometimes life has different plans."

Two months later, life threw me a curveball! I wasn't sure if I was more frustrated that Carole was right or the fact that my urologist called me and told me I needed to have surgery. I was diagnosed with prostate cancer four years ago, and it was time to have surgery with the goal of getting me back to being cancer-free. After 33 years as a teacher and school administrator, it became important for me to follow the advice of my doctor, my wife, and my daughter and focus on my health for the time being. The news from my doctor hit me hard, but with the support of my family and my years of having grit as an educator, I was able to turn the stress and anxiety caused by my pending surgery into an opportunity to spend my time focusing on my health and reflecting on my career. I had faith that God had a plan for me. I was committed to being a good patient and following my doctor's orders, and I used the time to reflect on my career and figure out what my next career steps would be. I still had a passion for being an educator and was committed to figuring out how I could continue to serve teachers and students, especially while I couldn't physically be in the schoolhouse.

At the same time, my daughter was entering her second year as an elementary school teacher. She had a wonderful experience in her student teaching and was well prepared to make a difference in the lives of her students. I'm sure you remember how hard the first year of teaching was. Hers was no different. After her first year, she asked me, "Dad, how did you make it so long? I am not sure I will be able to make it 30 years!" Each day, she told me about the challenges of her day, as she spent many hours each night and on weekends planning her lessons and activities for her students. She was so passionate about working with her students, but other things on the job were starting to take a toll on her. I consistently told my daughter to hang in there and tried to instill in her that she was an absolute blessing to her school and her students. I was proud that she found her own calling to be a teacher, and she knew I was there to support her. Giving her advice and supporting her inspired me to reflect on how I benefited from the support of some of my former administrators and how I was always focused and determined to show support for my teachers as a school leader. I was committed to helping her to love her job and have the same level of joy that I had after 33 years.

My daughter helped me reflect on how I tried to help my teachers through their various challenges during my career. I was empathetic with my daughter's challenges and was determined to help her, though there were most likely thousands of teachers going through similar challenges. While many were resilient enough to overcome the challenges of the heavy workload, after-school meetings, and the pressure of meeting the diverse needs of their students and parents, many teachers decided to move on from teaching. My daughter inspired me to research ways to help her and look at the current state of teachers. I had a chance to reflect on my friends who were teachers in South Africa and in the UK. I wish I were surprised to see that much of the data showed there was a glaring problem in education that is as bad today as it has ever been: teacher burnout. Too many teachers are getting burned out by the job, causing them to leave education altogether or leave for another school. If my daughter decided to leave education, it would be an incredible loss to her school and her students, and I was dedicated to seeing how I could help her and as many teachers as I could!

I always did my best to support my teachers throughout my career and asked myself, "How can I help serve teachers who are struggling to find joy in teaching, causing them to become burned out?" This book is dedicated to my daughter, who inspired me to write this book to help teachers overcome the challenges of being a teacher. Every time she tells a story about one of her little ones, her eyes light up! How can I help her never lose that and have the resilience that will lead her to a joyful career?

Throughout my career, I have experienced several challenges that have made me question if education is the right profession for me. I learned from my experiences and the support of my leaders and colleagues to be resilient and focus on the important role I had as an educator and not to be discouraged by the parent complaints or the amount of paperwork that my supervisor and district assigned me. This book is an honest depiction of the challenges teachers face and proof that if you invest in yourself, you too can have a joyful and fulfilling teaching career like I did. This book aims to affirm the important job you have and let you know that you are needed to help develop our next generation of leaders. This book provides 8 action steps you can take that will help you have a well-balanced life that will lead to you being the best version of yourself, inside the classroom and beyond. This book provides some useful information and some great tips that can help school administrators personally and in their efforts to support their teachers.

I hope you get as much enjoyment out of this book as I did writing it!

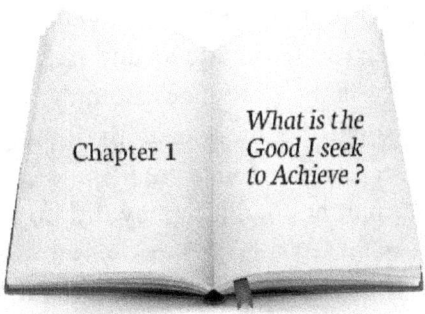

Chapter 1

"Joy, rather than happiness, is the goal of life, for joy is the emotion which accompanies our natures as human beings. It is based on the experience of one's identity as a being of worth and dignity."

– Rollo May

Amy dreamed of being a teacher since she was a young girl. She loved school and had a wonderful experience thanks to the teachers and coaches who loved, nurtured, and challenged her. She was excited to follow in her parents' footsteps, who were both teachers; her mom was a first-grade teacher, and her dad was teaching high school Social Studies. Amy's excitement to become a teacher led her to graduate from one of the top education universities, where she had hundreds of hours of practicum experience and student teaching. Amy was excited and more than prepared to enter the field of teaching!

After her first year at Sunshine Elementary School, Amy's excitement transformed into complete exhaustion! Amy knew her first year would be a challenge and thought she was ready for it, but she was overwhelmed by the amount of paperwork, time spent in meetings, and how much of her time was spent on managing her students' behavior. She was spending countless hours working in the evenings and on weekends, and the stress of the job was impacting her health. She felt completely overwhelmed, and her confidence in her future as a teacher was undermined.

Amy survived year one and prayed that her summer vacation would relight her fire and bring her passion as to why she got into teaching. Amy was convinced that she was a perfect fit for teaching and pledged that she was ready to give it one more shot. She knew she could lean on her parents' many years of experience for support! In the back of her mind, Amy thought that if things didn't get better in year two, her time and effort may be better suited to doing something else.

Amy tried to be resilient throughout her second year, but the challenges she faced didn't get any better. She loved her students and had a good relationship with the teachers at her grade level, but the challenges from the workload continued to affect not only her morale but also the morale of the other teachers. Amy knew the problems were bigger than just hers. Nice emails and coffee from parents were not making up for the critical parent emails as they did in year one, and the amount of time she spent working outside of school hours was impacting her health and social life. The day-to-day pressures created another long and stressful school year, and by the end of the year, Amy couldn't imagine doing this for the next 30 years. She felt trapped, like a hamster on a wheel, not going anywhere. She believed she was called to be a teacher, to love, nurture, and challenge her students and feel the excitement when her children learned something they never thought they could, but unfortunately, the job was taking a toll on her, and unfortunately, the bad outweighed the good.

Amy decided to leave teaching after only two years! She was seeking a better work-life balance and a place where her efforts would be appreciated. She decided to leave education and take a job at a local clothing store. She believed it would be a better job for her and that it would be easier for her to meet the demands of the job. In addition, the salary and benefits were close to the same as when she taught, except she would now get paid overtime if she worked more than 40 hours. She was looking forward to a better work-life balance and didn't have to take any work home after her 7:00 to 3:00 work hours, Monday through Friday.

Unfortunately, there are a lot of stories like Amy's, and it has been and continues to be a common trend worldwide that passionate and well-trained teachers are leaving the profession. Highly qualified teachers who have spent years preparing for their craft and are positive role models for their students are leaving the profession for many reasons. School districts and local school administrators continue to report the challenges of hiring and maintaining qualified teachers. Schools and school districts have tried various strategies to attract and retain teachers, but these strategies have not solved the root issue of teachers not feeling valued. Teachers need to feel valued and respected for the knowledge, skills, and experience each teacher brings to the profession. Teachers cannot be made to feel they are just filling a teaching slot, where the support they receive is "one size fits all." Teachers cannot be made to feel they are just a "cog in the wheel" that follows the assembly line and can be easily replaced. If your knowledge and skillset are easy to replace, how can you feel valued?

Have you ever declared to yourself or a colleague, "ALL I WANT TO DO IS TEACH!" Like you, or most of you who have your hand on this book, teaching was most likely a calling for you, not just a job. I hold this to be true that most teachers enter the profession to love, nurture, and challenge children so that they grow to love learning and grow up to be curious, kind, and generous adults. Teachers take the responsibility of building the next generation of leaders and do their part to ensure the well-being of their community and nation. Teachers enter the field to serve their students and partner with their administration and their families to prepare their students to be life-long learners and leaders in our global community. It breaks my heart to see so many teachers who had a heart for children and a heart for their craft get burned out and leave the profession!

The following provides some insight into the state of the global teaching profession:

- February 22, 2024, UNESCO (United Nations Educational, Scientific, and Cultural Organization), in its "Global Report on Teachers," revealed an urgent need for 44 million primary and secondary teachers worldwide by 2030. This includes a demand for seven out of ten teachers at the secondary level and a need to replace over half of the existing teachers leaving the profession. Sub-Saharan Africa is especially affected, with an estimated need for 15 million new teachers by 2030.

- According to the National Foundation for Educational Research (NFER), in 2022/2023, the UK is currently facing a critical teacher retention crisis, with a significant number of teachers leaving the state-funded sector, highlighting a major concern for the quality of education; the most recent data shows over 40,000 teachers leaving in 2023, representing around 9.6% of the teaching workforce, which is slightly higher than pre-pandemic levels. Schools in England are posting a significantly higher number of vacancies compared to pre-pandemic levels, indicating increased teacher turnover.

- According to the UK Department of Education (DfE), teacher vacancies in England have more than doubled in the past three years, from 1,100 in November 2020 to 2,800 in November 2023.

- According to recent reports, India faces a significant shortage of teachers, with over one million vacant teaching positions, particularly in rural areas, as per a NITI Aayog report in 2023; this translates to around 15% of all sanctioned teaching posts being vacant, with the most critical need in states like Uttar Pradesh, Bihar, and Madhya Pradesh.

- According to UNESCO data in 2024, Sub-Saharan Africa faces the most severe teacher shortage globally, requiring an estimated 15 million new teachers by 2030 to achieve universal primary and secondary education, highlighting the region's critical need for educators to meet growing student enrollment; this figure includes both new positions and replacements for retiring teachers leaving the profession.

  - This shortage significantly impacts the quality of education, as high student-teacher ratios limit individual attention.
  - Central African Republic, Chad, Mali, and Niger are identified as having the highest need for primary school teachers.

- The National Center for Education Statistics reported that 16% of U.S. public school teachers and 18% of private school teachers did not return to their school the following school year. Included in the percentage is approximately 8% of teachers who left their school for another school. The other percentage includes retirement and teachers who leave for better work-life balance and better compensation. (NCES: December 13, 2023)

- A Gallup Poll in 2022 reported that almost half of K-12 teachers feel burned out at work "very often." In the 2022 Gallup Poll on occupational burnout, 44% of American K-12 teachers reported feeling burned out often or always.

- A survey of 3,621 members of the National Education Association (NEA) revealed that 67% of these leading educators consider burnout to be a "very serious" issue. Meanwhile, 90% of the respondents think it to be a "somewhat serious issue" faced by educators. This survey attributed unfilled vacancies to be one of the major reasons for increased stress on the teachers and other staff. (2022)

- The Wall Street Journal reported in a 2022 poll by the National Education Association that 55% of teachers reported plans to leave the education field sooner than planned. Just one year earlier, in August 2021, only 37% of teachers reported this same feeling.

- The Wall Street Journal reported that at the beginning of 2022, data from the National Center for Education Statistics found that 44% of public schools posted full or part-time teaching vacancies due to unforeseen resignations and forceful reliability on non-teaching staff. That means nearly half of all American public schools were actively seeking new teachers and, meanwhile, were short-staffed.

- According to a survey by EdWeek Research Center, about six in every 10 teachers, 60%, experience job-related stress either always or frequently. This survey revealed that this job-related stress had effects on their sleep cycle, ability to enjoy time with family and friends, and physical health. As a result, 41% reported that their efficiency at work goes down when they get stressed. Only 9% of the teachers surveyed reported not or rarely feeling any stress. (July 2021)

The reality is that leaders in education around the world believe that you can't have a great school without great teachers, but teaching is an incredibly difficult job. The demands placed on teachers continue to grow. While COVID-19 had an impact on educators everywhere, other issues continue to be issues that jeopardize the morale of teachers, including compensation, safety, student management, and lack of opportunities for teacher training. These, and many other factors, contribute to low teacher morale, which leads to teacher burnout and teachers leaving the profession.

I applaud school leaders' efforts to attract and retain teachers by raising teacher pay, providing signing bonuses, and many other creative solutions like providing planning time at home. The challenge is that most of these strategies provide short-term gains in teacher morale but are not sustainable. In other words, teachers signing bonuses, merit pay, or providing rewards for Teacher of the Month can positively impact teacher morale, but they are not the long-term answer to address teacher attraction and retention. I believe there are tremendous opportunities for educational leaders to address this issue by ensuring each teacher, at all levels, feels like a valued partner in the educational process.

Focusing on providing incentives or professional development to improve a teacher's skills is appropriate and meaningful. But to truly make teachers feel valued and have a sense of joy, there must be a partnership and a personal investment in the teacher so that they feel valued and can truly be the best version of themself professionally and personally. When teachers are made to feel loved and valued and feel their worth is identified based upon who they are rather than what the end-of-year evaluation states, then and only then can a teacher have a sense of joy and fulfillment that can be sustained. Teachers who are valued and have confidence in their purpose as teachers can have a long-standing, joyful career. If teachers have the opportunity to invest in themselves and feel valued, they will remember: 'WHY' they became teachers in the first place and will be less likely to burn out. This is the key to retaining teachers and the key to having great schools!

The most successful schools and school leaders have invested time and energy into their teachers and have given teachers a voice about their teaching schedules, the curriculum they teach, and the professional development they receive. There needs to be an investment in developing the "WHOLE TEACHER," and the teacher needs to be empowered and feel valued as part of the education process. We must recognize that when schools hire teachers, they don't just get the teacher's math skills and knowledge of content and pedagogy. The school gets the teacher's values, personality, interests, and experiences. In other words, the school gets the "WHOLE TEACHER."

> *"After all, teachers come to work every day with themself.*
> *They don't leave their true- self in the car."*

This is the critical reason for this book and where my focus was as a teacher and school leader. I always prided myself in supporting my teachers, and the result was consistent teacher retention at each school I served. Administrators need to recognize that the schools should not be a dictatorship where teachers view administrators as the sole authority but as partners in the process of producing students who are curious, generous, and kind. By empowering teachers and investing in them personally, the outcomes are joyful and happy teachers, happy children, and a successful school. My book will provide you with strategies and activities you can do to protect your emotional well-being and sustain joy in your personal and professional life. I believe you can be successful and sustain your joy throughout a long and successful teaching career!

The goal is to support teachers and help them achieve joy and a healthy work-life balance. If teachers are joyful, they will stay in the profession and develop the best schools in the world. If joy is the goal, how can it be defined?

"Joy is the holy fire that keeps our purpose warm and our intelligence aglow."

– Hellen Keller

Joy and happiness are often used interchangeably, but there are distinct differences. Joy is often described as a more stable feeling that is less dependent on external conditions. Rather than being triggered by particular events, joy is a sense of inner fulfillment or peace that can exist even during difficult times. For example, people may find joy in acts of kindness, a sense of purpose, or deep personal connections, regardless of life's challenges. While happiness may be a reaction to external factors, joy is seen as a choice or outlook, a sustained sense of positivity that endures the ups and downs of daily life.

> *"Finding joy is probably tantamount to finding yourself and being comfortable in your own skin."*

> – Morgan Freeman

Happiness is generally understood as an emotion, a feeling closely tied to external events, circumstances, or achievements. Nick Saban's idea of happiness is:

If you want to be happy for a short period of time, you can:

- *Eat a steak to be happy for an hour.*
- *Play golf to be happy for a day.*
- *Go on a cruise to be happy for a week.*
- *Buy a new car to be happy for a month.*

Nick Saban implied that you could have quick indulgences that can provide temporary happiness, maybe an hour, a day, a week, or even a month. But while these indulgences lead to temporary happiness, they do not lead to sustained fulfillment, which can be defined as joy. I believe that for teachers to achieve a level of sustained fulfillment, there needs to be an intentional focus on having joy. As the American psychologist Rollo May stated, "Joy is the goal of life." If you want to achieve the goal of joy, you have to focus on how to be joyful.

In this chapter, I will give you permission to take ownership of the development of your own joy and your own morale and give you the strength to overcome the inevitable challenges that come along with teaching. I believe that while administrators around the world have good intentions and are doing great things, they have little chance of solving the problem of teacher retention without teachers having a firm foundation of confidence, resilience, and grit. Successful administrators foster a work environment and create a culture that helps teachers be resilient and become partners to help teachers own their morale. After you read this book, you will have your very own toolkit of resources and knowledge that will help guide you toward the work-life balance you desire. The following 8 chapters are filled with strategies and activities that are designed to help you focus on yourself, and I believe this will lead you to more joy and fulfillment in your classroom and beyond!

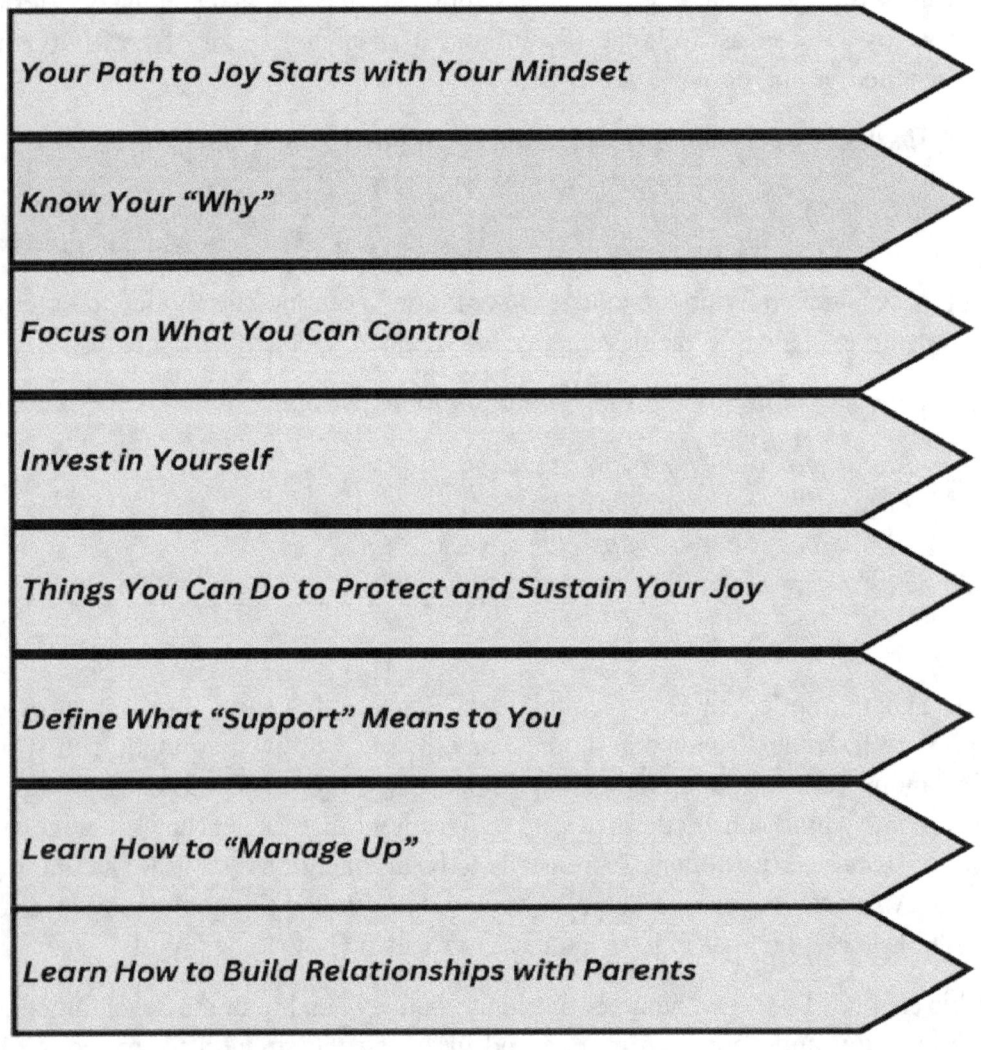

Your Path to Joy Starts with Your Mindset

Know Your "Why"

Focus on What You Can Control

Invest in Yourself

Things You Can Do to Protect and Sustain Your Joy

Define What "Support" Means to You

Learn How to "Manage Up"

Learn How to Build Relationships with Parents

"We are shaped by our thoughts. We become what we think. When the mind is pure, joy follows like a shadow that never leaves us."

– Buddha

Essential Learning Points

1. Schools around the world are challenged with attracting and retaining highly qualified teachers.

2. The key to attracting and retaining highly qualified teachers is to value teachers by investing in their skills, knowledge, and, most importantly, their joy.

3. The good I seek to achieve in this book is to develop teachers who have the knowledge and skills to protect their emotional well-being and live a life of joy in their professional and personal lives.

4. If the goal is to have joyful teachers, then we must be intentional in building and sustaining joy in them.

ACTIVITY 1

Over the course of a week, list the things you spend the most time doing and what percentage of your week you are engaged in that activity. Then, put an asterisk or highlight the things that excite you or bring you the most joy. For example, you can grade papers, have dinner with family, go to church, read a book, walk your dog, golf, etc. The goal is to identify the things that bring you the most joy.

_____

_____

_____

_____

_____

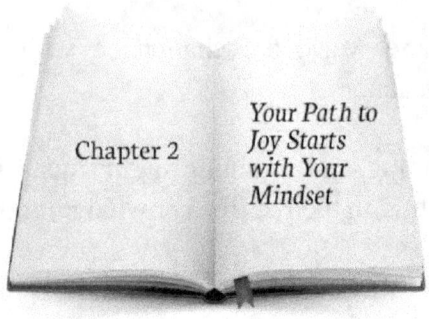

Chapter 2

Your Path to Joy Starts with Your Mindset

"Be the change that you wish to see in the world."

– Mahatma Gandhi

Tom serves as the Math Department Chair at Wilson Secondary School and has taught 9th-grade Algebra and Honors Algebra for the past 8 years. Tom's director called a meeting with his team of 9th-grade teachers to let them know that Bob, one of his math teachers in his department, had recently taken medical leave and would miss the remaining four weeks of the semester.

His director alerted him and his team that finding a qualified sub would be difficult this time of year, so the responsibility to provide instruction for Bob's classes would fall on him and the other 5 math teachers in the department. Tom was relieved that Bob was expected to have a full recovery. Although Bob couldn't physically deliver the curriculum, he was able to provide some guidance on the lesson plans and consult on the needs of his students.

Tom was an up-and-coming superstar at Wilson Secondary School because of his "whatever it takes" attitude. He loved math and loved his students. His positivity and joy for teaching came from his experience and his positive attitude. When Tom was a young student, he was diagnosed with attention deficit disorder. Primary school was very hard for him, and he didn't receive the appropriate support until ninth grade. He was committed to making sure his students had more support than he had when he was younger and was motivated to make the world better for his students and the students at Wilson Secondary School. Tom's reason for being a teacher provided him with the determination and positivity to meet the needs of his students and the students in his school, no matter what.

When Tom met with his team, he was prepared to deliver a "win one for the Gipper" speech to motivate each member of his team.

In 1928, head coach of Notre Dame football, Knute Rockne, delivered this famous motivational speech to his players during halftime against the undefeated Army team. Tom knew his team needed to be motivated and knew that some of his team would do whatever it would take to cover Bob's classes. He also knew that some members would complain if they were asked to do anything in addition to their teaching duties and responsibilities. Tom told his team that he had a similar experience his first year at the school, and the team pulled together to make sure the students were afforded an excellent learning experience, even in the absence of their teacher. Tom then asked a couple of teachers to come up with a plan to execute the lesson plans and assess each student's performance. Tom would work with Bob to develop the final exam for the class. The teachers worked out a plan to ensure Bob's five periods were covered each day. Tom's team was prepared to take on all the duties to show support for Bob and his students. Tom's team followed his lead with a positive attitude during the last four weeks of the semester. At the end of the semester, the director at Wilson Secondary School was proud of the work of Tom's math department, and there was not even one complaint about the extra work. Tom's director gave him and each team member a $1,000 stipend as a "thank you" for their commitment to Bob's students and the school. The director told Tom it was because of his resilience and positive leadership; his teachers accomplished the task and did not complain one bit.

Tom's attitude was a tremendous asset to his school and his team. Having a positive mindset is the first step in your path to joy. I believe there are three critical components to creating and sustaining your positive mindset:

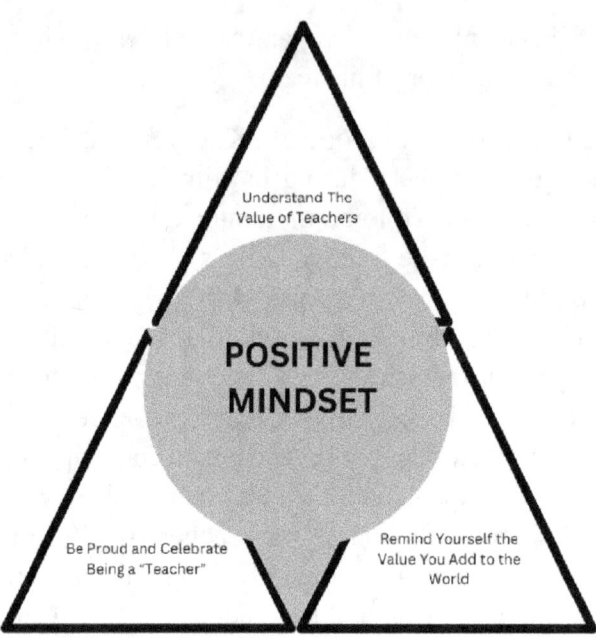

1. Understand the Value of Teachers and Teaching: In addition to growing students academically, teachers play a crucial role in supporting students' emotional and social well-being. I still remember the time I was feeling pressured by my baseball coach to give up basketball and focus solely on baseball. I didn't want to disappoint my basketball coach or baseball coach, but at the end of the day, I loved playing all three sports. I remember sitting in Coach Pidcock's office and asking for his advice. He was my football coach and told me not to feel the pressure from the coaches and that if I had fun playing all three sports, then play all three. He cared about what was best for me, and I knew I could count on him for honest advice. I ended up playing three sports in high school and enjoyed all three seasons.

The importance of teachers cannot be overstated. Teachers shape the minds of future generations and have a direct impact on their school and school community as a whole. Their influence reaches far beyond the classroom, leaving an indelible mark on the world.

"But I always come back to the fact that being a teacher is one of the greatest jobs in the world, and sometimes the people who have chosen to walk that noble path simply need to be reminded that there is a vast army of educators and grateful citizens who have their backs. Someone needs to remind teachers that they are clearly loved!"

-Taylor Mali, 2012

Taylor Mali is an American Slam teacher and a huge advocate for teachers, and the quote came from his book titled "What Teachers Make." I remember coming across his slam poetry years ago, which led him to write a book that had a tremendous impact on me.

Here is an excerpt of Taylor's rant that went viral on YouTube back in 2009. His book would come along three years later.

A dinner guest who was an attorney made this comment: *"What's a kid going to learn from someone who decided his best option in life was to become a teacher?"* *He continued that it's true what they say about teachers, "Those who can do, do, those who can't, teach." Taylor had enough, and here was the last half of his response to the attorney's question, "Tell my Taylor, what do you make?"*

You want to know what I make?

I make kids wonder,
I make them question,
I make them criticize,
I make them apologize and mean it,
I make them write, write and write,
and then I make them read.

I make them spell definitely, beautiful, definitely, beautiful, definitely, beautiful, over and over again until they will never misspell either one of those words again.

I make them show all their work in math and hide it on their final drafts in English,
I make them understand that if you got this then you follow this, and if someone ever tries to judge you by what you make, you give them this.

Here, let me break it down for you,
So, you konw what I say is true,
Teachers? **Teachers make a difference!**

Now what about you?

I have consistently told my teachers that I never want to hear them say, "I'm just a teacher." They are so much more than that! I came across this poem written by Stacy Bonino that shows that a teacher's job is much more than teaching:

I am so much more than just a...**Teacher**

I am a **counselor and psychologist** to a problem-filled child,
I am a **police officer** that controls a child gone wild.

I am a **travel agent** scheduling our trips for the year,
I am a **confidante** that wipes a crying child's tears.

I am a **banker** collecting money for a ton of different things,
I am a **librarian** showing adventures that storybook brings.

I am a **custodian** that has to clean certain messes,
I am a **psychic** that learns to know that all everybody only guesses.

I am a **photographer** keeping pictures of a child's yearly growth,
When **mother and father** are gone for the day, I become both.

I am a **doctor** that detects when a child is feeling sick,
I am a **politician** that must know the laws and recognize a trick.

I am a **party planner** to celebrate holidays with all,
I am a **decorator of a room,** filling every wall.

I am a **news reporter** updating on our nation's current events,
I am a **detective** solving small mysteries and ending all suspense.

I am a **clown and comedian** that makes the children laugh,
I am a **dietician** assuring they have lunch or from mine I give them half.

When we seem to stray from values, I become a **preacher,**
But I'm proud to be these people because...
I'm proud to say, "**I'm a Teacher.**"

By Stacy Bonino

2. Remind Yourself of the Value You Add to the World: To have sustained joy as a teacher, you need to have the resilience or grit to constantly remind yourself of the value you add to your students, your school, and the world. Being resilient and having grit can help you overcome any challenges that come along with teaching and enable you to protect your emotional well-being and your joy. Grit is a mindset, a psychological trait that can be developed and grown. The Cambridge English dictionary defines grit as courage and determination despite difficulty. Leading psychologist and author Angela Duckworth wrote in her book; "Grit: The Power of Passion and Perseverance," (2016) that grit is "the single trait in our complex and wavering nature which accounts for success, even more important than natural talent, ability, and intelligence.

In an article in Forbes Magazine (October 2013) titled "Five Characteristics of Grit; How Many Do You Have?" Margaret M. Perlis describes five essential characteristics of Grit: courage, conscientiousness, follow-through, confidence, and excellence.

What is Grit?

1.Being Courageous	Your ability to manage fear of failure. Successful people who are gritty are not afraid to fail but see failure as a learning opportunity and part of the growing process. They understand that there are valuable lessons in defeat and that the vulnerability of perserverance is requisite for high acheivement.
2.Being Conscientious	A personality trait that describes someone who is responsible, careful, and thorough. Conscientious people are often organized, efficient, and able to exercise self-control and achieve their goals. They are also known to be good team players and diligent workers and adhere to norms and rules.
3.Having Follow-Through	Includes having long-term goals and endurance that provides the ability to follow through with the context and framework in which to find the meaning and value of your long-term efforts, which helps cultivate drive, sustainability, passion, courage, stamina, which leads to grit.
4.Being Confident	Allows you to get back on the proverbial horse as you stay focused on following through on your goals. It gives you the strength to overcome setbacks and stressors in the job, and gives you the strength to be resilient, and navigate any issues in your way.
5.Striving for Excellencee	In general, gritty people strive for excellence, and don't seek perfection. Perfection is someone else's perception of an ideal, and pursuing it is like chasing a hallucination. There are obvious challenges in teaching and the barriers to success. Excellence is an attitude, not an endgame.

Understanding that Grit is a mindset and something you can develop is a critical strategy to help you remind yourself how important you are to the teaching profession and your students. You must keep your morale upbeat. Tom was determined that he would help Bob's class, no matter how much pushback he got from some of his fellow teachers, and no matter how much additional work it added to his plate. Because of his experience and his grit, he knew it was something that could come along in the teaching world, and he was confident he could handle it. Understanding and accepting the importance of reminding yourself how valuable you are is vital to staying positive when times are tough and knowing that your purpose as a teacher is far greater than any issue you may face.

3. Be Proud and Celebrate Being a "Teacher": If you were to research the most respected professions in your country, where would teaching rank? The World Economic Forum reported on January 15, 2019, that Teachers were listed in the top 10 of the most respected professions in the world, along with doctors, lawyers, engineers, and police officers. This data is consistent with research done in the US, UK, India, and many other countries. From the beginning of time, Education has been a cornerstone of human development and the evolution of education stems from ancient times, where the focus was on hunting and gathering. It has evolved to current times, where we are navigating digital platforms and how to utilize artificial intelligence effectively. The pillar of educating our youth and instilling the values and knowledge of culture and period of time has always been our teachers. History tells us the importance of teachers!

If I had my list of "most respected professions," I would also include the criteria of "most important professions." My list would consist of professions that help mold, shape, and save lives. I would include- surgeons, first responders, our military personnel, and all professions that have a direct impact on the lives of people and a community. You better believe that "Teacher" is at the top of my list! If you can name one self-made successful adult who did not have one teacher, coach, or director have a significant impact on their life, you can stop reading right now. My purpose in this book is to convince you that teaching is one of the most noble professions and that by permitting you to be proud of your calling and take ownership of your positive mindset, you will live a much more fulfilled and enjoyable life, professionally and personally.

I challenge you to think of someone who helped mold you and helped shape your life. For me, I can't name the doctor who brought me into this world, but I will always be grateful for my surgeon, who gave me a new lease on life after curing me of cancer. Also at the top of my list is Mr. Watson. He was my seventh-grade Algebra teacher who noticed that I was pretty good at math. He changed my trajectory in math and gave me confidence that no other teacher did. He helped to shape my life, and I still feel his impact today. Part of a positive mindset is celebration, and I found a way to celebrate Mr. Watson.

In March 2020, I had an article published in **"My Forsyth Magazine"**, titled *"The Little Things Make You Feel BIG"*:

Recently, I volunteered to drive my daughter to West Long Branch, NJ, for her second semester at Monmouth University. On our trip, I decided to do something that I had only considered doing on my past trips up north. While walking my puppy at a rest stop in Virginia, I called Mr. Watson to see if he was available one morning for breakfast or lunch to catch up. He shared he was available Saturday morning at 10:00 and then he was attending the Penn basketball game at the old Palestra.

Mr. Watson was my 7th-grade Algebra teacher at Clearview Regional Junior High School in Mullica Hill, NJ, back in 1980 something. I was a typical 13-year-old who loved sports and my friends, but Junior High was just ok. I was a quiet kid with a lot of confidence on the football and baseball fields but very little in the classroom. One fall Friday, we were anxiously waiting to get our unit test scores back and nervous to see how our scores would impact our weekend. As Mr. Watson shuffled into class, his typically jovial personality that poked out of his maroon turtleneck sweater appeared to be very serious. After an awkward moment of silence, he announced, "I spent all night grading your tests, and there was only one perfect score." I immediately asked my buddy Eric, "Why is he so serious, and why was this such a big announcement? It was probably Thom, Erin, or Chucky!" While most of my friends were congratulating one of the brainy kids in the class, Mr. Watson was walking very slowly in my direction. I was in complete shock when he looked at me and said, "Great job, Eddie!"

When I finally got over the initial shock that I had the highest grade, I was a little embarrassed that Mr. Watson called me out in front of the class. Some students had a shocked look on their faces, but my friends were quick to tell me, "Great job!"

I had always been good in Math, but the lesson I learned that day went way beyond academics. I learned that "People may not always remember what you did, but they will always remember how you made them feel." That day, Mr. Watson made me feel very special. He could've just passed the graded tests back and not said anything, but he chose to do something special that this middle-aged man still remembers more than 30 years later.

When I sat with him on that cold Saturday morning at the diner, I thanked him for the confidence he instilled in me, and we reminisced about his teaching career (and my student career) for the next hour. I will admit he stole some of my childhood when he let me know the reason he wore a turtleneck sweater. Every day, he wore a turtleneck sweater to play along with the student rumors that his head was cut off in the Army and that the turtleneck did hide the scars where his head was sewn back on. He related to his students better than any of my other teachers in 7th grade and was totally invested in his students' success.

I share this story because, like you, my life is very busy, and I rarely take the time to thank my teachers and coaches for the impact they have made in my life. I have been so fortunate to have some of the kindest and loving teachers at Clearview and they played a big role in my decision to become an educator. My hope for you is that you take advantage of any opportunity to thank a former teacher or coach by sending a handwritten note, making a phone call, or taking them to lunch. In addition, if your child has a teacher who is having a positive impact on him or her, send the teacher a note of gratitude.

When I said goodbye to my friend, Mr. Watson, he smiled and told me how fortunate he was to have such a wonderful teaching career and he was lucky to have made so many friends in his years at Clearview. That day, I was the fortunate one! I can't remember the grade I received in his class and forgot most of the Algebra he taught me, but I will always cherish the relationship I had and still have with Mr. Watson. Plus, I have a deeper appreciation for turtlenecks.

"The most overlooked or 'taken for granted" profession that has the most profound impact on shaping the lives of people on a daily basis is… TEACHING."

My hope for you is that you never discount the importance of what you do, and I hope that you are constantly reminded that you are truly one of our nation's heroes. Ironically, on the day I wrote this chapter, I noticed the new price sheet on my barber's mirror. The note at the bottom of the new price sheet caught my eye and made my day:

HEROE DISCOUNTS ($2.00 off any services) for:
MILITARY, POLICE, FIRE, EMT, EDUCATORS
Thank you for your service!

Thank you, Aysel and Gino, and Jackson Barbershop, for acknowledging teachers as the heroes that they are!

Essential Learning Points

1. A positive mindset is the first step in your path to joy!

2. There are three components to sustaining a positive mindset in teaching:

   o R 1. Understand the value of teachers and teaching,

   o R 2. Remind yourself how valuable you are to the world and

   o R 3. Be proud and celebrate being a teacher

3. The purpose of a teacher is much greater than any challenge that teachers face.

4. Teaching is one of the most respected professions in the world.

Testimony

After teaching high school English for five years, I was transferred to another school within the district. Despite the unexpected change, I remained committed to maintaining a positive mindset and determined to gain the trust of my new colleagues, department chair, and administrators. Although my new assignment was still within the same district, the school had different departmental expectations, including a strong emphasis on English grammar. While I fully supported the department's grammar program, implementing it in my classroom proved challenging and felt like just another task added to my already overwhelming schedule.

Like most English teachers, my true passion lay in reading and discussing literature—few embraced grammar instruction with enthusiasm. It was often seen as dull, complicated, and arbitrary. However, my new school prided itself on a high college acceptance rate. Since the SAT included a strong grammar component, students needed to be well-versed in concepts such as sentence fragments, misplaced modifiers, and subject-antecedent agreement.

Implementing the grammar program presented significant challenges. The textbook was not only dry but also incomplete, providing scant explanations with minimal examples. It failed to explain the reasoning behind grammar rules, which I believed was essential for students to fully grasp and retain the concepts. Additionally, many students expressed frustration, claiming they had been "learning" the same grammar rules since first grade yet had retained little. This motivated me to develop my own lessons tailored to ensure true internalization of the rules and their practical applications.

I devised ways to make each concept stick through graphics, mnemonic devices, and simple explanations. I created flowcharts to illustrate the relationships between verbs and objects, used humorous sayings to help students remember conjunction types ("correlative" conjunctions have "relatives" and come in pairs), and demonstrated how apostrophes often replace missing letters (you are = you're). The time and energy I devoted to making grammar more accessible paid off in many ways. My students began noticing errors in printed materials and advertisements, eagerly bringing them to class to share. This practice evolved into a game, reinforcing the realization that not everything in print is correct! Their grades on weekly grammar quizzes improved, as did their interest in understanding why an answer was right. What they once dismissed as a tedious subject became something they genuinely engaged with.

Though starting over at a new school was challenging, I was confident that determination and a positive mindset would benefit both me and, most importantly, my students. Whenever you enter a new school or work under a new leader, you can never be sure what expectations will be placed upon you. However, by embracing challenges with a positive mindset, you can transform any obstacle into an opportunity for growth.

- Amy Price, retired teacher and administrator

ACTIVITY 2

I'll bet you can name at least one teacher, off the top of your head, who helped shape your life, who noticed when you lost your front tooth, lent your lunch money when you forgot your lunch, or was a shoulder to lean on, when you had to make a tough decision on what college to attend.

ACTIVITY 2A. Make a list of the teachers that you remember who helped to shape your life. What did that teacher do to make you feel special?

_____

_____

_____

ACTIVITY 2B: If you were organizing a dinner party at your house, which former teachers or current colleagues would you invite and why?

_____

_____

_____

_____

_____

ACTIVITY 2C: Write a letter to your teacher and thank him or her for playing a positive role in your life. If you have children, write a handwritten note to your child's favorite teacher.

_____

_____

_____

_____

_____

_____

_____

Chapter 3 — Know Your "Why"

"We don't get burned out because of what we do.
We get burned out because we forget why we do it."

– Jon Gordon

In my 30-plus years, I wish I had a dollar for every time I heard, "Must be nice to be a teacher; you get your summers off," or, worse, the old saying, "Those who do, do; those who can't, teach." These comments can be incredibly frustrating because they reflect a lack of respect for the teaching profession. Remarks like these, combined with the immense pressure placed on educators today, certainly take a toll on our morale. But we must remember that people—especially some parents and community members — think they understand what it's like to be a teacher simply because they went to school. Just because you went to school doesn't make you an expert.

Once you commit to developing a positive mindset, the next step in your journey toward joy is to remind yourself why you chose to teach in the first place. Remembering your "why" and being able to articulate it clearly to others is a crucial step in maintaining both professional fulfillment and personal happiness.

Simon Sinek's influential book "Start with Why" (2009) emphasizes that every individual should begin by understanding their WHY—the purpose, cause, or belief that drives them. He argues that our "WHY" gives our work meaning and connects us to a deeper sense of purpose beyond the daily grind of long school days, exhausting weeks, and fleeting summers. When you are clear about your "WHY," you become less reliant on external motivators like money or recognition. Instead, your motivation and joy come from within. Sinek also asserts that understanding your "WHY" helps you navigate difficult periods, overcome obstacles, and build determination and hope. Rather than being weighed down by the daily demands of the job, you remain focused on the bigger picture. Knowing your "WHY" doesn't just sustain motivation—it leads to greater job satisfaction and overall joy.

For me, discovering my "WHY" provided clarity, direction, and a strong foundation throughout my career in education. It served as an anchor during difficult situations and gave me the strength to push through even when I was exhausted from working 80-hour weeks. More importantly, understanding and articulating my "WHY" has enabled me to help many teachers and administrators rediscover their own purpose, rekindling the passion and enthusiasm they had when they first entered the profession—recognizing your "WHY" is an essential step on the path to joy in teaching.

I am excited to share my "WHY":

After spending four and a half years in college, I graduated with a degree in Political Science and was contemplating law school. I had no immediate plans or job lined up and was searching for something to pay the bills and keep me occupied. A friend encouraged me to apply for a job as a counselor at the school where he had worked for the past two years.

The school was a transformational institution for boys who had been through the court system and were found guilty of truancy, drug distribution, or, in some cases, gang-related violence. The students, ages 14 to 18, came from all over the country, from Delaware to California and many states in between. The school primarily recruited staff with college athletic experience, and my six-foot-four, 215-pound frame certainly didn't hurt. There were no bars or chains—only the trust that staff built with the students to create a safe environment and prevent escape attempts. While rare, students occasionally did try to run, so counselors and staff needed to be physically prepared to intervene. Upon arriving on campus, I quickly realized I was one of the smallest staff members responsible for the safety and well-being of nearly 1,000 students.

I worked in a unit named after Abraham Lincoln, which housed 32 students. Most boys remained at the school for 12 to 18 months, and our unit had eight staff members responsible for their care around the clock. At the time, I was engaged and had to coordinate schedules with my future wife, as my days off were Monday and Tuesday while hers were the more traditional Saturday and Sunday.

My work schedule was 4 PM to midnight, Wednesday through Saturday, and 8 AM to 4 PM on Sundays. The upside? I had a stretch of time off from Sunday at 4 PM to Wednesday at 4 PM. I enjoyed my new role, working closely with the eight students on my caseload, ensuring their success academically and athletically while helping them earn career certificates that could change the trajectory of their lives.

One of my most memorable students was Fred, a 15-year-old from western Pennsylvania. He was the first student to arrive after I joined the school, and he quickly became one of my favorites. When Fred arrived, he was nervous and shy, leaning on me for support as he adjusted to his new environment. I built a strong relationship with his mother, and together, we worked to give Fred the best chance at success—one that would break the cycle of incarceration that had already claimed his father and older brother.

But Fred presented me with a significant challenge: changing his mindset. I'll never forget the day he told me, "Ed, I appreciate you trying to get me an education and a vocation, but I can make more money in an hour selling drugs than I would working at McDonald's for a month." Even more concerning, he wasn't afraid of going to prison because his father and brother were already there.

I was determined to connect with Fred, knowing that one day, he would return to the same environment that had led him to our school in the first place.

As time went by, I found myself coming in on my days off to take Fred and the students on my caseload out to lunch, bowling, or a movie. I believed in rewarding my students for positive behavior rather than threatening them with punishment when they did not meet my expectations. I quickly discovered that every Sunday morning, when I arrived at work at 8:00, Fred would be waiting for me with his chessboard. The boys were allowed to sleep in until 9:00 on weekends— but not Fred on Sundays.

As I watched Fred and my other students progress in the program and connect with me, I started to believe that education just might be for me. One day, a co-worker confronted me and said, "Ed, you're wasting your time with these kids. A white man cannot earn the trust of black students. And you're wasting your time coming in on your days off—we all get paid the same amount."

Wow. That was over thirty years ago, and I still remember it like it was yesterday. As shocking as Eric's statement was, it made me reflect on my career and question whether I was truly making a difference. But seeing Fred waiting for me each Sunday and witnessing the relationships I built with my students was eye-opening. It motivated me to be the best mentor, counselor, and coach I could be. I felt like I was making a difference.

My vision for my students was to love them and prepare them to be responsible citizens—better sons and future husbands. For some, I needed to break the cycle of a dangerous mindset: "I'd spend a third of my life in prison if it meant I could live the other two-thirds with the money I made selling drugs."

What I saw in Fred and my other boys were children who wanted to be loved, who needed someone to believe in them and give them a fighting chance. Yes, I knew there were racial and socioeconomic differences between us, and my students knew that, too. But we had the same goal. I didn't come in on my days off because I had nothing else to do—I did it because my boys needed me. And, in a way, I needed them. They gave me purpose. I worked hard to prepare all my students to re-enter society, not just serve their sentences at Glen Mills.

Fred was one of my younger boys and quickly became an ideal student. He excelled academically, participated on the weightlifting team, and earned a certification in art design and screen printing. After a year, his mother was ready for him to come home, and Fred had crossed all his T's and dotted all his I's. He was prepared for success, and I felt confident he was ready to return to the same environment he had left. When Fred was promoted out of our school, I beat my chest and thought to myself, "Job well done."

Fred motivated me to go back and get my teaching certificate because he helped me find my passion—growing young people. He taught me that my purpose was to help others and love my neighbor, regardless of race, ethnicity, socioeconomic status, or religious belief.

Months passed, and my students at Lincoln Hall kept me busy. I had spoken with Fred's mother a few times since he left, and she said he was acclimating well back at his old school. But one day, my world changed.

I walked into work, and my team leader handed me a letter. It was from the Pittsburgh State Penitentiary. I held my breath as I opened it and read:

Dear Ed,

I hope you are good and that Darnell is behaving. I'm sorry to tell you this, but I messed up real bad. I got myself into a terrible situation. A couple of my boys and I robbed a gas station, and one of my friends shot and killed two of the workers. I'm sorry. I wish I had listened to you. I don't know what's going to happen to me, but I miss you and thank you for everything you did for me. I wish I had listened to you better.

Fred

Even now, I still tear up reading that letter. And this—this is my "**WHY**."

I am motivated by the reality that no matter how much I pour into a child, no matter how much attention I give, no matter how much time I spend—there is always more I can do. I admit there were tough patches in my career, and sometimes, there were places I would have rather been. But not once did I fail to give everything I had to love, nurture, and challenge every child under my supervision.

Fred is my "**WHY**." And he is not unlike any other child—he just wants to be loved and given a chance to succeed. All students deserve that. Teaching was never just a job for me; it was my calling.

More than thirty years later, I still think about Fred and the impact he had on my career. Fred, along with my other students at Lincoln Hall, motivated me to be the best mentor, counselor, and teacher I could be. He set me on the path that led to a lifelong career in education. While I learned my "**WHY**" from Fred, I have learned from the hundreds of teachers I've worked with over the years that every educator has their own "**WHY**." What is yours?

1. Love children and have a passion to serve.

2. Had a wonderful experience and loved school.

3. Had an awful experience and are determined to make it better for the future generation.

4. Had a love for a subject and want to spend their time talking about history.

5. Had a teacher who had a profound impact on their life, and they want to pay it back.

6. Fell into teaching for other reasons like they came from a family of educators.

Throughout my career, I have interviewed hundreds of teachers, and I'll admit—I never focused much on their college grade point average or where they graduated from. What truly mattered to me was their "why." Why did they choose to become a teacher?

This may sound arrogant, but I consider myself a master teacher. I could train someone to deliver curriculum effectively, integrate technology into their lessons, and provide remediation for students who needed extra support. But what I couldn't teach was heart. Either someone had a heart for students and a passion for teaching, or they didn't. No amount of training could change that.

I would tell every teacher I hired:

"At our school, we don't simply teach math, coach basketball, or direct the play—we teach, coach, and direct children. Teaching is personal."

I want you to reflect on your "why." When someone asks what you do for a living, never say, "I'm just a teacher." Own who you are. Be proud of your purpose. And don't be afraid to share your "why."

When people ask me what I do for a living, my answer is always the same:

"I am a difference-maker for my children—all of them—because that is what I am called to do!"

Essential Learning Points

1. Knowing your "WHY" is a critical second step in your path to joy.

2. Knowing your "WHY" protects your positive mindset by helping you reflect on your purpose, cause, and belief that drives you.

3. Knowing your "WHY" can get you through difficult times and challenging situations.

4. Being able to articulate your "WHY" can help your colleagues when they are becoming burned out: remember "that people don't burn out because of what they do, they burn out because they forget why they are doing it." (John Gordon)

Testimony

My name is celestine Minoo Mutinda, I am 34 years old, kenyan by birth and currently working at the kingdom of Eswatini with Heart for Africa organisation. I was born and raised in a remote village back in Kenya. I am the third born in a family of 4. I have one sister and two brothers. I was born in one of the most archaic family governed traditions because I found myself in a family with no male figure around. This is because my mother had been married off to an older barren woman who desperately wanted a younger woman to sire babies for her. This tells you that I do not have a father and have never met any father figure for the 34 years that I have lived. By God's grace I grew up in that very poverty striken environment until the age of two 4 when this particular woman, (the one who had married my mother) passed on. Two years down the line when I was only 6, my mother also passed away. It was this time that life became even harsher.

The long and short of this aftermath is that we were rejected by both relatives and neighbours, a situation that forced the local government to intervene by forcing my maternal relatives to accommodate us. This was the beginning of another torture to say the least. We were segregated from everyone in the homestead, we were denied food, we slept outside in bushes and denied the opportunity to get an education.

In all this, I did not know that God still cared and saw our situation. Through a good samaritan, my 3 siblings and I ended up in a children's home (Mully Children's Family.) Our lives began thriving, I started school and through the support of my amazing teachers, I loved school and did well. I met amazing teachers who not only taught me but also showed me love and compassion. With time, I healed from my childhood trauma because I was surrounded by teachers who encouraged me, loved me and assured me that If I worked had in my studies, I would be able to take care of myself and other people in the future.

My teachers were the first people that made me really understand the power of education. I was so desperate to work hard so that I can run away from the kind of background I was coming from. Needless to say, this was the conception of my desire to become, not just a teacher, but a good teacher. I saw how powerful teachers are when it comes to transforming the lives of the learners and I knew that is exactly what I wanted to do. I wanted to impact lives positively, I wanted to encourage learners coming from difficult situations and assure them that there is hope. I wanted to be a world changer through teaching. I wanted to be able to give back to the community, through educating children, and for me this also meant using teaching to give my gratitude back to God for saving my life, for allowing me not to succumb to the torture that I went through as a very young girl, to thank God for giving me a second chance in life even when relatives had given up on us.

Today, as a teacher at Project Canaan Academy, I am living my dream. I am in the happiest space of my life. The children that I interact with everyday have been through hard situations before being rescued by heart for africa and my role is to make them understand that It does not matter where they are coming from, God saw them and brought them to safety for His glory. I am indeed thankful that I became a teacher and that God led me to the children at Heart for Africa. Every day I normally ask Jesus to lead me and teach me how He wants me to lead and teach these children. They make me complete.

Everything in this world happens for a reason and I am thankful for my past because it shaped my future and that is why I am more than happy in the teaching ministry.

Thank you.

-Celestine Minoo Mutindo
Head Teacher Heart for
Africa Eswatini, Africa

ACTIVITY 3

In the space below, write your "WHY." This is the second action step of your personal portfolio and your path to Joy!

_____

_____

_____

_____

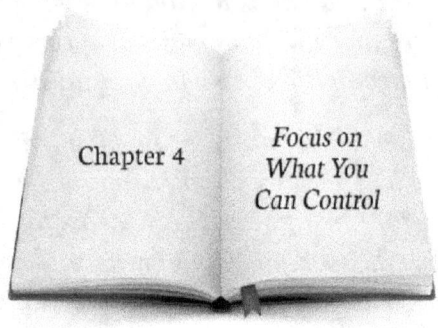

Chapter 4

*Focus on
What You
Can Control*

*"What we can control is our performance and our execution, and that's
what we're going to focus on."*

– Bill Belichick

The earliest educational systems can be traced back to the ancient governments of China and Egypt, where agreed-upon curricula reflected the values of their communities. In China, under the Xia dynasty, education focused on literature, archery, and rituals. In early Egypt, the emphasis was on religion, writing, mathematics, architecture, and science.

Throughout history, educational systems in Europe, Asia, and Africa were established either by government agencies or the church, each setting specific standards for what was to be taught and learned.

Education in America dates back to the early New England colonies. In 1647, Massachusetts became the first colony to pass a law regarding education, requiring any town with 50 or more families to hire a teacher who could instruct children in reading and writing. At that time, all teachers were expected to follow the four fundamentals of teaching:

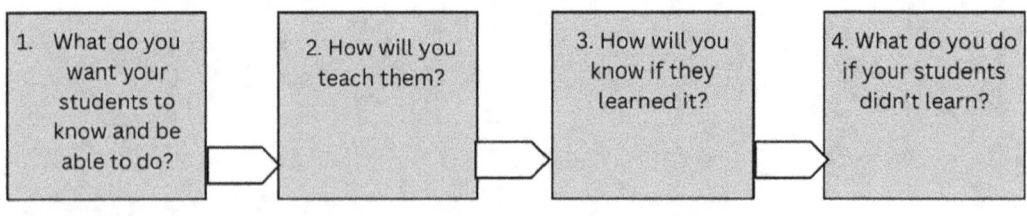

1. What do you want your students to know and be able to do?

2. How will you teach them?

3. How will you know if they learned it?

4. What do you do if your students didn't learn?

Over the past 350 years, expectations for teachers have grown more complex. However, the four basic fundamentals of teaching have remained unchanged for thousands of years. Today, teachers are expected to do more than ever before: How will you differentiate instruction to meet the needs of all students? How will you incorporate technology? How will you accommodate students with disabilities? And in some cases, how will you ensure students pass college entrance exams? No matter how complex a lesson plan may be, I firmly believe that good teaching always comes down to these four fundamental components.

In education training programs, the core principles of good teaching are instilled in future educators. Many programs include student teaching experiences that allow aspiring teachers to practice lesson planning and execution. Teachers are trained to focus on meeting the diverse academic and emotional needs of their students. When I began my career, I intended to base my lesson plans on these four core components while incorporating my own style and creativity. However, I quickly realized that teaching involves far more than what happens in the classroom. Countless factors outside my control took up my time, forcing me to learn the hard way that I needed to focus on what I could control in my teaching. Here's an example of how Jim learned to focus on what he could control.

Jim felt great after his interview for a high school social studies position. Confident that he understood what he was signing up for, he eagerly joined the team at Rumble Secondary School. Having just retired from the military, he was excited about the structure of his second career— school hours were set from 7:30 AM to 3:30 PM, semesters lasted 18 weeks, and summative assessments were built into each nine-week period. He was assigned five sections of ninth-grade history, given his own classroom, and provided with all the necessary supplies for the school year.

As Jim prepared for his first year of teaching, he looked forward to implementing his lesson plans. After completing pre-planning the week before school started, Jim was ready to begin the year. He had mapped out the first two weeks of lessons, including activities and assessments designed to keep students engaged from bell to bell. His plans were structured around 50-minute class periods, each with an engaging opening and closing activity. But when Jim arrived early on the first day, he was caught off guard—the bell schedule had been altered for the first three days due to an administrative decision to implement Advisement time. The purpose of Advisement was to help students, especially new ones, adjust by providing information about schedules, extracurricular opportunities, and behavioral expectations. Jim didn't dwell too much on its importance—he was more concerned about losing eight minutes from each of his 50-minute classes for three days.

Additionally, he had overlooked the fact that he was required to stay at school until 9:00 PM on Thursday for a parent night. Jim realized that while he thought he was prepared for his new profession, he was realizing that he wasn't.

Determined to stay ahead, Jim used the weekend to adjust his lesson plans for the second week. He also made a conscious effort to shift his attitude and adopt the mindset that he needed to be flexible. In the military, expectations had always been crystal clear, and communication from his superiors had never been an issue—this new environment was a major adjustment.

Eager for a fresh start, Jim arrived at school early Monday morning, ready for week two. However, as he entered the building, he immediately noticed something was off—the hallway lights were out. When he reached his classroom, he discovered that the school had lost all power due to a batch of severe thunderstorms the night before. The building, constructed in the early 1970s, had very few windows, making the classrooms and hallways nearly pitch-black. Since Jim was the first to arrive, he headed to the main office to wait for the principal or any other administrator.

When the principal arrived, Jim joined him and the head maintenance supervisor to inspect the backup generator in the electrical room. To their shock, they found that the generator had been struck by lightning and was completely burned out. Jim asked, "What do we do with the students when they arrive in 45 minutes?" Typically, the school's protocol for power outages was to rely on the backup generator. Unfortunately, there was no plan in place for what to do if the generator failed. As more teachers began arriving, the principal gathered a small group—including Jim—to brainstorm a solution. Jim suggested guiding all students into the gym, the one area with the most natural light. The plan was to keep them there until the maintenance team and city workers restored power.

Jim's principal appreciated his quick thinking and the cooperation of the staff. However, after learning that power wouldn't be restored for another three hours, the principal made the decision to cancel school for the day. He then asked Jim to help develop a plan for safely dismissing students and staff.

Driving home, Jim felt a sense of accomplishment, knowing the principal had relied on him to help manage the crisis. Yet, he couldn't shake the thought: Will I ever have a normal week where I can just teach?

As teachers, we understand that many things are beyond our control—power outages, bell schedules accommodating Advisement, pep rallies, and assemblies.

We are also aware that countless other disruptions can impact a school day, from dedicated testing days to decisions made by district and school leaders—not to mention the unpredictability of Mother Nature. Inclement weather and election days can cancel school, and students getting sick can interrupt the delivery of a unit.

While Jim was focused on his students' test scores and ensuring he delivered the state's curriculum, his colleagues didn't ease his concerns when they informed him of additional responsibilities he hadn't considered. These included:

- Bus duty and/or lunch duty

- Proctoring the SAT

- Coaching or sponsoring a club

- Staying after hours for parent nights

- Chaperoning student dances

- Supervising field trips

Jim quickly realized that even the best-laid plans often require adjustments. He also learned that teaching came with far more responsibilities—and required much more flexibility—than he had initially anticipated. However, the most valuable lesson he learned was this:

"Although he couldn't control everything that impacted him (or his class), he was in control of how he responded and how he let those things affect him emotionally."

The third action step in Jim's path to joy was learning to focus on what he could control. Instead of viewing Advisement as an obstacle, he began to see it as an opportunity to connect with students and help them feel more prepared for the school year. By shifting his perspective, both he and his students benefited emotionally.

"Focus on that which you can improve, correct, or change. Ignore what you can't control. Focusing too much on things beyond your control will negatively impact those things that are within your control."

— Coach John Wooden

Research supports the importance of focusing on what you can control. A 2015 HuffPost article, How to Stop Worrying by Cliff Hsia, reported that 85% of the things people worry about never happen. Of the 15% that do occur, 79% of people find that the difficulty is easier to handle than expected or that they learned something valuable from it. This suggests that 97% of worries are ultimately unnecessary.

Melanie Greenberg, a clinical psychologist and author of The Stress-Proof Brain (2017), believes that while moderate worrying can be beneficial, excessive worrying can cause anxiety, overwhelm, and make it difficult to take action or solve problems.

When I was a young teacher, my principal advised all new teachers to focus on what they could control. It sounded simple, but what I wasn't told was that this is a skill—one that, when developed, serves as a powerful safeguard for maintaining a positive mindset. While we can't always control what happens to us, we can control how we respond. By focusing on what's within our control, we not only become better teachers but also protect our mental and emotional well-being, ultimately leading to greater joy in the classroom and beyond.

Coaches use this same principle to help athletes perform at their highest level. A tennis coach, for example, spends hours refining a player's movement, stamina, serve, backhand, and forehand. If a player spends too much time worrying about winning, the weather, or their opponent's ranking, it diverts energy away from their development. In tennis, some factors—such as the opposing player, the wind, and the official's calls—are beyond the player's control. However, peak performance and success become much more attainable when athletes focus on what is within their control.

The same applies to teaching: Focus on what you can control.

I have compiled a list of 16 things you can focus on to become the best teacher possible. By centering your attention on these areas, you'll strengthen your positive mindset, improve your teaching, and build resilience. In turn, this will help you sustain your joy in the profession while also enabling you to better navigate the unpredictable challenges that inevitably arise.

1. Your Attitude

Wake every day with the attitude that "Today is going to be an amazing day!" This was not always automatic for me, but an area where I faked it until I made it. Do whatever it takes to get going, whether it's your favorite coffee, an early jog or walk in the morning, talking to your best friend, or listening to a motivational podcast on the way to work. My choice is always sports radio, 94WIP, from Philly, and I always had more of a pep in my step when my football team wins. Prepping your attitude leads to things you can do at school that will make a difference every day: show up early, ready to go, say hello to everyone in the hallway, and stand at the door to welcome your students with a big smile. When people saw me (especially my students), I wanted to give off the vibe that I was a positive person and ready to seize the day. I recognize, and it's not easy, that some people don't always say "good morning" back. All I can control is how I respond to them, not how they respond to me.

2. Lesson Planning

Create clear objectives and activities that will utilize your personality to provide learning opportunities for your students. Use your creativity to design lessons that engage your students to make learning fun. Some teachers are highly skilled at lecturing, while some are more skilled at storytelling. While all teachers are accountable for the same learning standards, the activities, strategies, and assessments you use don't have to be the same. Don't feel the pressure to create every lesson. Teachers are always willing to share their ideas.

3. Classroom Environment

Set up your classroom to be orderly and establish routines that reinforce your expectations for your students. Design bulletin boards that create a positive classroom atmosphere. Post student work throughout the class, make visible the learning objectives, and promote learning to your students.

4. Student Management

Implement classroom expectations that foster a respectful learning environment by rewarding specific positive behavior; "thank you for raising your hand" and "great job listening." Post positive class norms in your classroom for expected behavior. I always liked to list the expected behavior versus a list of all the rules of the class. I learned early in my career that students see that rules are made to be broken and norms as things they need to comply with. I would make sure I communicated (either in a syllabus, posted in the classroom, or in a letter home to parents) the behavior expectations for my students. I always believed in stating what the expected behavior was rather than just listing the rules. For example:

IN MY CLASS, ALL STUDENTS ARE EXPECTED TO:

1. Practice good manners!
   a. Respond "yes" or "no" to questions and never say "na", "nope", or "yea" and if you didn't get the question, say "excuse me" and not "what".
2. Be respectful to other students in how you speak and avoid foul language and words that can hurt someone.
3. Wear appropriate clothing that is respectful to the learning environment.
4. Raise your hand if you have a question and listen when others speak.
5. Ask for help if you need it.
6. Be respectful with technology and you have permission to text before and after class.

You can have as many expectations as possible if you'd like, but I usually try to limit my list of expectations to 10.

5. Assessment Strategies

Create formative and summative assessments that adapt to your teaching style and the learning styles of your students. To assess your students' learning, you can use True/False responses, multiple choice questions, projects, portfolios, essays, and many other strategies that measure your students' understanding of the content. It can be effective to provide your students with some choice in what assessment they will demonstrate their learning best. After all, you are measuring what your students have learned, not how well they can do on a certain test. For example, giving your students 10 minutes to complete 5 equations doesn't always measure if they know how to solve the equation, but it does measure how fast they can solve them. Be aware that some students don't do well on timed assessments.

Dr. Thomas R. Guskey is an incredible resource for assessing learning. One of my favorite quotes of his is:

"We don't assign grades to students; we assign grades to performance. And just as performance is always temporary, grades, too, should always be temporary."

– Guskey, 2021

6. Feedback and Grading

Develop opportunities to give students feedback on their performance and progress. Don't feel the need to assign a grade to everything. Students will learn from making mistakes on rough drafts and will benefit greatly from your feedback and guidance. Communicate clearly to your students how you will provide feedback and how often. In addition, it is important to clearly communicate how your student's performance will be measured and the established grading criteria for any project or test.

"Grades improve learning only when accompanied by specific guidance and direction from the teachers on how to improve. A score and grade at the top of a paper does nothing to help students improve."

- Thomas R. Guskey & Susan M. Brookhart.

7. Instructional Pacing

In many cases teachers have to keep pace with their team or the school's pacing guide, but in some cases, you have flexibility on spending more time or less time on a lesson or unit. You have control of how much time and opportunity you provide your students who need remediation and acceleration. Some students may need additional time on certain content, or advanced students may have already mastered some content which you could provide them enrichment activities.

8. Learning Activities

Don't be afraid of using your creativity and trying some new activities. Ron Clarke got the attention of his principal, but sure connected to his students. Design and execute activities that engage your students in their learning. Examples could include group work, Socratic seminars, experiments, or hands-on experiences. I always told my teachers that I wanted to see the students working harder in the classroom than them.

9. Student Encouragement

Encourage students to participate in their learning and foster a learning environment that helps students build confidence and grow to love learning. Younger students sure do love stickers and there's nothing like a hand-written note to send home to mom and dad. I know it may be 'old school, but those notes still end up on the fridge. Getting to know your student's interests and activities after school will connect you with your students. Theodore Roosevelt said it best when he said, "Students don't care how much you know until they know how much you care."

10. Use of Resources

Selecting resources outside of the school-required textbooks and using creative educational tools to enhance learning enrich learning for your students. I still remember when I was in 5th grade. My class traveled up the turnpike in New Jersey to see where George Washington and his troops crossed the Delaware River on Christmas night in 1776. It was much more engaging than the lecture by my teacher.

I know teachers spend a lot of their own money to purchase supplies for their classrooms. Don't be afraid to ask your supervisor for some funding. You may be surprised that that funding is available and plus, you have nothing to lose.

11. Communication with Parents

I've dedicated an entire chapter to help you with this. Having proactive communication with parents can make your life much easier. It includes letting parents know how you will be communicating throughout the school year and helps you set clear expectations on how they can communicate with you. I recommend not sending any emails to parents from 4:00 Friday afternoon to Monday morning unless it's an emergency. By sending emails on the weekends, you are letting parents know you are available to them on the weekends. You control protecting your personal time.

12. Relationships with Parents

Building positive relationships with your parents is a positive strategy that can make your job a lot easier. Being proactive by sending home positive notes about their child helps offset the time when you have to call when their child misbehaves. It also helps when you tell parents how excited you are to have their child in your class at Open House, and nice notes home build leverage when you need help or support in your classroom. Invite your parents to be guest readers or provide other opportunities for parent engagement, like career days or to help with school parties.

13. Substitute Teacher Plans

Make sure you have sub plans for at least three days with activities that can be used any time throughout the year so that if you have an emergency, you don't have to worry about having to create plans. If you have a planned absence, you should update your sub plans with activities that support the unit of instruction. No matter whether teaching in public or private school, you should be allotted a certain number of sick/personal days. Don't feel guilty about taking one!

14. Your Willingness to Collaborate with Others

If you are a new teacher, be open to accepting a mentor, and if you are a veteran teacher, be open to mentoring a new teacher. Collaboration leads to forming positive relationships that will result in collaborative planning of lessons, including assessments, and an emotional support structure for everyone. You can control how much effort you put in.

15. Your Participation in Sponsoring or Coaching Programs Outside the Classroom

If you have a special interest in a sport or club, serving as a coach or sponsor can be very rewarding and help you earn additional money. It is a great way to get to know students outside of class. Even if you are not an official coach or sponsor, attending student activities, like dances, further shows that you are invested in your students. Your students will notice if you are in the stands at their volleyball game, and so will their parents!

16. Your Confidence in Asking for Help

I used to think that asking for help was a weakness. I was trained to prepare my lessons, manage my students, close my door, and do my job. I was amazed at just how lonely it could be teaching in a school if I isolated myself. When I was a young teacher, I was nervous to ask for help. I found myself planning my lessons alone and eating lunch alone. I only lasted one year in that school. Asking for help from others builds relationships and shows others that you are a team player and that you value the person you are asking for help from. When people ask me for advice, I am always willing to help. Asking others for help can make them feel needed and valued. Educators, by nature, are most willing to help.

The things I listed for you are just some of the things you can control that can help you build your confidence and protect your positive mindset when you are at school. If you find yourself in any challenging situation or challenging conversation, ask yourself, "What am I in control of?" You will find that you are in control of more than you realize. If you're in control of a situation, take the appropriate action steps to respond to the situation and if you are not in control of it, remember you are still in control of how you respond to it.

Essential Learning Points

1. What you focus on gets the most attention.

2. Spend time focusing on the things within your control.

3. Spending too much time worrying about things outside your control can cause anxiety and unnecessary emotional stress.

4. You can't always control what happens to you, but you can control how you respond.

5. For each situation, ask yourself what is within your control.

Testimony

Thinking back on my first year of teaching, I faced many challenges. Being a first-year teacher already came with enough anxiety—creating lesson plans, managing student behaviors, adapting lessons for students who were behind grade level as well as those who were far beyond, communicating with parents, and more. On top of that, I had the added stress of a "revolving door" in my classroom.

Within the first three months of the school year, I had been observed about ten times. These informal observations were conducted by the school literacy coach as well as administrators. It often felt like someone was coming in daily to watch me and take notes on what I was doing. While I knew observations were a normal part of my job, as well as theirs, it still felt like I wasn't meeting expectations or doing something right.

The feedback I received was always positive and encouraging, yet as a first-year teacher—and a perfectionist—I still put immense pressure on myself to improve. These thoughts consumed me, causing me to worry constantly about things beyond my control.

After many days of self-doubt, I took a step back and reflected on my first few months as a new teacher. For the first time, I realized all the small accomplishments I had overlooked—earning the trust of my students and their parents, building a strong classroom community, fostering academic growth in all my students, and supporting their development as individuals. The list went on.

Once I recognized everything I had achieved, the anxiety of being observed disappeared. My mindset shifted from "Oh no, who is coming in to watch me now?" to "Come in and see what we're doing today!"

While college teaches you how to create lesson plans and instruct students, it doesn't prepare you for the thoughts many educators have about not doing enough. In the world of teaching, countless factors are beyond our control, but it's crucial to recognize even the smallest accomplishments that are in our control—and to celebrate them.

— Ann Spurka, 1st Grade Teacher (Second Year)

ACTIVITY 4

ACTIVITY 4A: Make a list of the things at your school that are within your control and the things that affect you that are outside your control.

CONTROL

_____

_____

_____

_____

_____

_____

OUTSIDE YOUR CONTROL

_____

_____

_____

_____

_____

ACTIVITY 4B: Pick two things you are not in control of at school and would want to have more control. Why would you want more control, and are there things you can do to gain more control?

_____

_____

_____

_____

_____

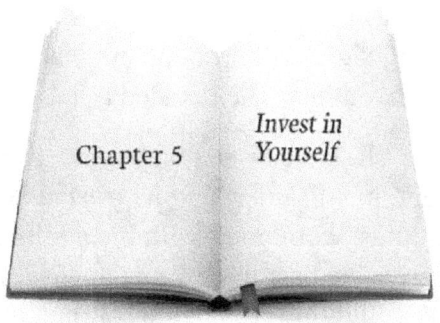

Chapter 5

Invest in Yourself

"You can't just sit there and wait for people to give you that golden dream. You've got to get out there and make it happen for yourself."

– Diana Ross

John is entering his 20th year of teaching and currently serves as an 8th-grade English teacher at Cambridge Primary School. A dedicated and highly regarded educator, he has also been a member of the principal's advisory council for the past five years, representing the 6th-grade teachers. John has benefited from working under a stable administration, which has been in place for the past decade. Known for his teamwork and leadership, his principal has come to rely on him as a key member of the school community.

This year, in addition to his lead teacher duties, John was asked to teach a new course. After the first month of the school year, he found himself spending three hours each night and several hours on weekends preparing lessons and grading assignments. His family quickly noticed a change— he was more irritable, exhausted, and not quite himself at home. One weekend, John's wife reluctantly shared her concerns, and her words hit him hard. He felt like he was failing—not only as a teacher but also as a husband and father. That Sunday night, for the first time in his career, John experienced a sinking feeling in his stomach about starting the new week.

John had an excellent relationship with Laura, his principal, and he recalled something she had said during her first meeting with the staff:

"If you ever feel a pit in your stomach on a Sunday night or anxiety on the drive to work Monday morning, come see me and give me a chance to help you."

She understood the warning signs of burnout. John had never imagined he would find himself in that position, but now, he decided to take her up on her offer.

When John met with Laura, she encouraged him to talk through what was weighing on him. She was an exceptional listener, and he trusted her. He explained that the pressure of his teaching duties, combined with his additional responsibilities, had become overwhelming. Over the past three years, he had been asked to lead a new committee each year—now juggling leadership roles on three committees, serving on the Principal's Advisory Cabinet, and spearheading the school's latest initiative, one-to-one technology. On top of all this, he was adjusting to teaching a new course.

For the first time, John admitted he was questioning his own abilities. He felt stretched too thin and unsure of what he was truly good at anymore. Maybe, he thought, it was time for a change.

Laura immediately recognized how much was on John's plate and was determined to help. He was a tremendous asset to the school, and she didn't want to lose him. She responded with empathy and encouragement, asking him,

"Where do you find the most joy in your job? And is there a role within the school that would allow you to achieve a better work-life balance?"

John hesitated. He wasn't sure. With so many commitments, he had lost sight of what he excelled at—teaching. Fortunately, Laura had an idea.

She offered John the opportunity to attend training for the Highlands Ability Battery (HAB), an assessment designed to help individuals align career choices with their natural abilities, leading to greater job satisfaction and performance. Laura had taken the HAB years ago and found it transformative. She believed it could help John gain clarity and rediscover his strengths.

Desperate for a solution, John agreed.

The four-hour HAB assessment was followed by a two-hour consultation to review his results. What John learned would not only reshape his career but also help him grow into a better version of himself—both at work and at home. His key takeaways included:

- **He thrived as a Specialist** – He excelled when he could focus on one task or project at a time. Managing multiple unrelated projects drained his energy. The numerous committees and initiatives had been taking a toll on his emotional well-being.

- **He was a strong introvert (90%)** – He recharged through solitude but was constantly surrounded by people. Without intentional alone time, he was running on empty.

- **His greatest energy came from working with students** – The assessment reaffirmed that teaching was his true calling. While he had been considering a move into administration or another role, he now realized that being further removed from the classroom would not align with his "why"—the reason he entered education in the first place.

For the first time in years, John felt like he had real answers. The HAB provided insight that no well-intentioned administrator's feedback had ever fully articulated. He finally understood why he had been feeling so frustrated, and it validated that teaching was exactly where he was meant to be.

Excited to share his results with Laura and his wife, John felt a renewed sense of purpose. Over the next three months, Laura supported him in making key adjustments to restore his balance:

- **Focusing on leading his department and stepping back from most school-wide committees** – This allowed him to devote more time to teaching while continuing to lead the technology committee, an area of expertise and passion.

- **Scheduling intentional alone time twice a day** – Whether to collect his thoughts, plan his day, or recharge, he now understood the importance of carving out quiet moments without guilt.

- **Providing the HAB to his department's teachers** – Using departmental funds, John arranged for his colleagues to take the assessment, strengthening their team dynamic and helping them better understand each other.

- **Reducing the workload he brought home** – This gave him more quality time with his family, something he had been missing.

Through this process, John didn't just rediscover his passion for teaching—he learned how to create the balance he needed to thrive both professionally and personally. His journey served as a powerful reminder that sometimes, the key to fulfillment isn't a career change—it's a better understanding of ourselves.

Like John, I benefitted both professionally and personally from the HAB. Despite having nearly 25 years of experience in education, it wasn't until a leader recommended this type of professional development that I had the opportunity to participate. I was invited to join a cohort of leaders from across the state who aspired to become school superintendents. On the first day, I remember hearing, "This program will help you grow and allow you to determine whether the role of superintendent is right for you." This professional development wasn't just about learning the duties of a superintendent; it was designed to foster personal growth and ensure I was on the right career path.

When I took the HAB, I discovered that the superintendent role was not for me. Dr. Stiles, my HAB consultant, pointed out that I would thrive in a role where I could directly impact students and teachers. She noted that I would struggle with being far removed from daily interactions in an office setting. I was at my best when working in a school surrounded by students and educators. Thanks to Dr. Stiles and Dr. Harden, who led the program, I found greater joy and fulfillment by pursuing work that aligned with my personal strengths and natural attributes. The HAB also opened doors to new opportunities, including coaching and participating in mission trips, which deeply resonated with my servant's heart.

This chapter contains resources and strategies that will help you invest in yourself and develop a meaningful narrative to share with others. By prioritizing your personal growth, you build confidence and reinforce your "WHY"—the reason you became an educator. This is the next action step on your path to joy!

I have two fundamental questions for you:

1. How well do you really know yourself?
2. How confident are you in articulating who you are to others?

We've all been in situations where we had to introduce ourselves—starting a new job, joining a new team, or attending training with unfamiliar colleagues. In my experience, most people introduce themselves with a simple statement like:

"Hello, my name is Sarah, and I teach 5th grade at Sewell School."

Typically, people share their name and position. What they say next often depends on one of three things:

1. How nervous they are in front of new people.
2. How much time do they expect to spend with the group?
3. What the person before them said.

It's comfortable to introduce yourself by stating what you do, where you've worked, or accomplishments you've achieved. But my question to you is: do you ever share who you are— your natural attributes and what it's like to work with you? Have you ever shared your "WHY"?

If you're at a one-time seminar and will likely never see the people at your table again, keeping it simple is fine. But if you're joining a new team or stepping into a leadership role—such as a lead teacher or department head—sharing more about yourself is crucial. Your colleagues will spend a great deal of time with you, and an authentic introduction can be the foundation for strong professional relationships.

Imagine I was introducing myself as a new member of your team. Instead of just stating my role, I might say:

"Hello, my name is Ed, and I am excited to join your team. I come from Clearview Regional Secondary School and will be serving as the lead teacher for the History Department. A little about me: I am 95% introverted, which means I process things internally and may seem quiet in group settings—but that doesn't mean I'm disinterested. I am a nurturer, so if you need my help, I will first want to know how you are before discussing the task at hand. I process information logically and can feel overwhelmed if too much is thrown at me at once. I prefer face-to-face communication, but if you need to send an email, bullet points are much easier for me to process than long paragraphs.

I also have a creative mind, making me a strong problem solver with a lot of ideas. I am a family man and value a healthy work-life balance. I will never send emails over the weekend or during holidays unless it's an emergency. I am invested in each of you and the success of our department and school. You'll find me to be a dedicated team player."

You may not have encountered an introduction like this before, but I've found that being open and vulnerable allows others to see that getting to know me is important to me. It also signals that I am interested in learning about them personally.

On the other hand, I once had a new supervisor introduce himself by saying, "I know you don't know me or trust me, and I don't know or trust you yet, either."

This introduction did not sit well with me, and 15 years later, I still remember it as the worst introduction I've ever heard.

The details in my introduction weren't made up on the spot. They came from years of investing in my personal growth. I wanted to understand myself, articulate my strengths, and communicate effectively. Too often, we spend unnecessary time and energy figuring out how to work best with our teams. Imagine if we already had that insight—if we knew how each team member preferred to communicate and collaborate. Wouldn't it be beneficial if teams had shared norms and a common language to help them function at their best?

By investing in yourself and using the tools available, you can grow both personally and professionally while developing your personal narrative. With education becoming increasingly complex, tools that provide insight into your personality, communication style, and cognitive strengths are invaluable. They can be powerful resources for both individual development and team effectiveness.

I have been fortunate to use several tools that have greatly benefited me and the teams I've worked with. Personalized professional development—whether through personality assessments, strengths evaluations, or career alignment tools—can be transformative. These resources not only help refine your skills and interpersonal communication but also align your career with your natural strengths.

Each tool has the potential to support your personal growth, and I am excited to share several with you so you can invest in yourself.

ASSESSMENT	PURPOSE	OUTPUT	STRENGTHS
Highlands Ability Assessment (HAB)	Measures innate abilities and aptitudes to guide career and educational pathways	Detailed report and 1:1 consultation on strengths, weaknesses, and career recommendations	Focuses on natural abilities rather than personality traits
Myers-Briggs Type Indicator (HBTI)	Identifies personality types based on preferences in perception and judgement	Four-Letter type (e.g. ENTP, ISFJ)	Simple four-letter type for easy understanding

True Colors Test	Categorizes personality traits and communication styles using color-coded types	Primary and secondary color types	Easy to understand; effective for improving team dynamics and performance
Five Voices Assessment	Identifies communication styles and strengths within team settings	Primary and secondary "voice" for communication and teamwork	Useful for understanding team roles and improving collaboration
The Birkman Method	Assesses behavior, motivation, interests, and underlying needs for a holistic personality view	Comprehensive profile including a "Birkman Map."	Combines motivation, interests, and stress behaviors: useful for deep self-awareness and team cohesion

The Highlands Ability Battery (HAB)

"I tell people that when I sit there quietly when we are brainstorming, please don't think I am not engaged. I am quietly processing the answer or resolution, and when I have my answer, I will share it. I am not going to shout out possible answers like an extrovert."

– Edward J. Spurka

The Highlands Ability Battery is a comprehensive aptitude-based assessment that measures a range of natural abilities, including learning preferences, problem-solving styles, and specific talents. HAB's approach aligns with the concept that "innate aptitudes" remain constant over time versus skills like vocabulary, which can be improved with practice. The HAB is unique in its "Whole Person Model" for personal growth and development with its 8 Factors: Goals, Career Development Cycle, Abilities, Skills, Interests, Personal Style, Family, and Values.

EIGHT FACTORS

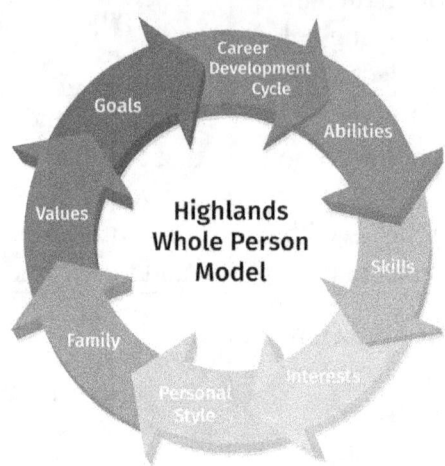

The HAB can be very useful for teachers and has been used in education for:

Career Planning	can guide teachers in aligning career choices with their natural strengths, enhancing job satisfaction and performance
Skill Development	identifies cognitive abilities that enable teachers to focus on developing skills aligned with their natural abilities
Leadership and Talent Management	helps schools and school districts identify employees with aptitudes for specific roles, aiding in talent allocation and succession planning

Another unique factor about the HAB is that the assessment report includes a one-on-one with a HAB consultant. For more information, you can go to https://www.highlandsco.com, or you can read the primary book associated with the HAB: "Don't Waste Your Talent: The 8 Critical Steps To Discovering What You Do Best" (McDonald and Hutcheson, 20217).

Myers-Briggs Type Indicator (MBTI)

The Myers-Briggs Type Indicator is one of the most widely recognized personality assessment tools used extensively in personal growth, team building, and career development. Based on Carl Jung's theories of psychological types, the MBTI was developed by Isabel Briggs and her mother, Katharine Cook Briggs, with the aim of making Jung's ideas accessible for personal and professional use. Jung theorized that people differ in four fundamental areas:

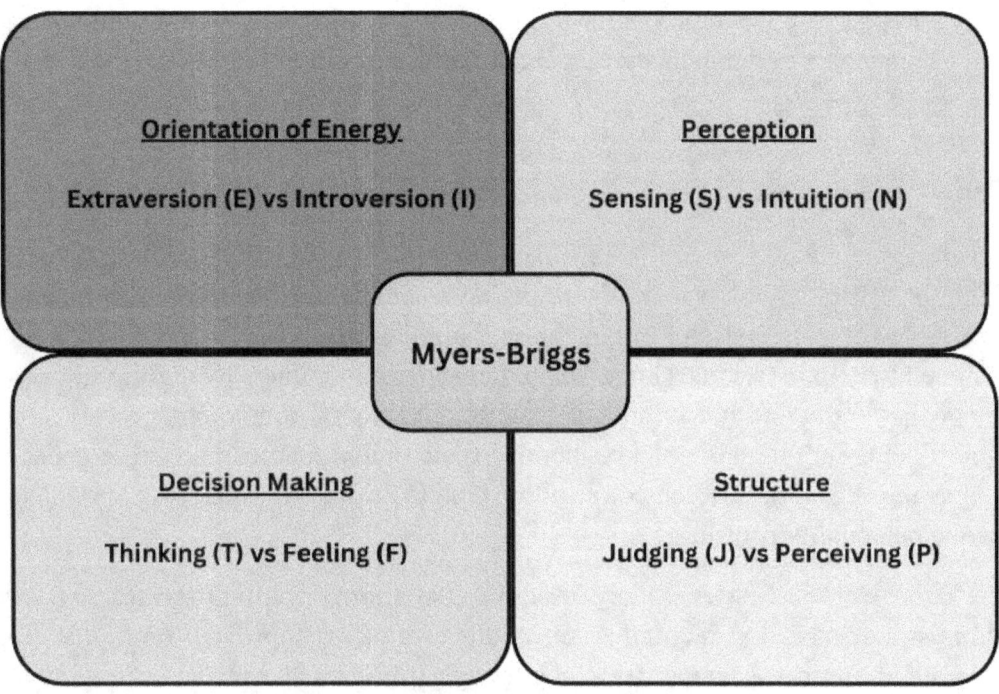

Isabel Briggs Myers and Katharine Cook Briggs expanded on these ideas, creating a framework to describe 16 personality types by combining one trait from each of the four dichotomies. For example, someone who prefers Introversion, Sensing, Thinking, and Judging would be classified as an ISTJ.

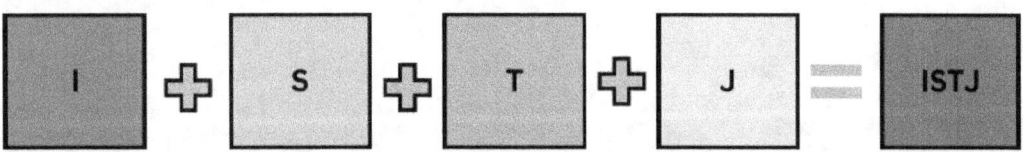

Each personality type represents a combination of preferences that influences an individual's behavior, decision-making, and interaction with others.

The MBTI helps individuals understand how their personality affects their work preferences and relationships. For example:

- Self-Awareness: MBTI promotes greater self-awareness by helping individuals recognize strengths and limitations within their personality type.

- Team Dynamics: Understanding personality types enables team members to appreciate diverse approaches, improving collaboration and reducing conflicts.

- Leadership Development: MBTI is often used in leadership training to help managers understand and leverage personality diversity within their teams.

True Colors Test

Developed by Don Lowry in 1978, True Colors builds upon the work of Carl Jung, Katherine Briggs, and Isabel Myers, using a simplified approach that makes it accessible for personal and organizational applications. The True Colors Test is designed to help individuals understand themselves and others by highlighting core personality traits and behavioral tendencies. By having a color framework, True Colors helps individuals quickly identify their own strengths and preferences as well as those of others. Each color in the True Colors framework corresponds to a unique personality profile.

The True Colors Test is widely used in educational settings for teachers and administrators. The test facilitates better self-awareness, improved communication, and collaboration for teams. By recognizing your own and other's strengths and preferences, you can enhance collaboration with other teaches, resolve conflicts as they arise more effectively, and create a more harmonious work setting.

BLUE	Reflects individuals who are empathetic, compassionate, and relationship oriented. Blues often prioritize harmony, teamwork, and understanding in their interactions.
GOLD	Represents people who value organization, structure, and responsibility. Gold personalities are typically reliable, detail oriented, and dedicated to their commitments.
GREEN	Indicates individuals who are logical, analytical, and focused on knowledge and competency. Greens often prefer data-driven approaches and are problem-solvers at heart.
ORANGE	Describes those who are spontaneous, energetic, and action oriented. Oranges are often adventurous, adaptable, and enjoy taking risks.

Five Voices Assessment

Five Voices assessment is focused on interpersonal dynamics and was developed by GIANT Worldwide, a leadership development company. Five Voices is based on the premise that individuals primarily communicate in one of the Five "Voices": NURTURER, CREATIVE, GUARDIAN, CONNECTOR, OR PIONEER. The Five Voices model aims to foster effective communication by helping individuals understand their dominant and secondary voices.

The Five Voices of Leadership

PIONEER: Are driven, goal-oriented, and focused on results. They tend to be confident decision-makers who enjoy leading and pushing for progress.

NURTURER: Are compassionate, empathetic, and relationship-oriented, often attuned to the feelings and needs of others. They value harmony and seek to support those around them.

GUARDIAN: Are detail-oriented, reliable, and focused on protecting resources and efficiency. They often excel in roles requiring structure and analysis, balancing risk with caution.

CREATIVE: Are visionary thinkers who are focused on innovation and potential. They often see the big picture and bring fresh, original ideas but may struggle with sharing ideas in a way others understand.

CONNECTOR: Are natural networkers and communicators who enjoy building relationships and bringing people together. They are skilled at motivating and energizing others.

The Five Voices assessment emphasizes improving communication, collaboration, and conflict resolution.

- Communication: By understanding one's dominant voice, individuals can become more conscious of their communication style and how it impacts others.

- Team Dynamics: Teams using the Five Voices framework can develop a shared language, reducing misunderstandings and fostering the appreciation of diverse perspectives.

- Conflict Resolution: The assessment helps individuals recognize potential communication clashes, enabling proactive conflict management.

THE BIRKMAN METHOD

The Birkman Method is a psychological assessment tool designed to help individuals and organizations gain insights into behavior, motivations, interests, and the underlying needs of individuals. Developed by Dr. Roger Birkman in the 1950s, The Birkman Method has since evolved into a widely used instrument in various settings, including personal development, career coaching, leadership training, and organizational development. Unlike other assessments that solely identify personality traits or communication styles, The Birkman Method delves into the "why" behind behaviors, offering a holistic view of an individual's unique patterns, stress triggers, and interpersonal needs.

The Birkman Method consists of two main components: a personality and social perception questionnaire. The assessment covers four key areas:

1. **Usual Behavior:** captures how individuals typically behave when they are at their best. This includes observable behaviors such as communication style, assertiveness, and openness to collaboration.

2. **Underlying Needs:** identifies an individual's hidden needs or the conditions required to maintain their optimal performance. These needs are often internal and may not be readily visible to others, yet they play a crucial role in determining how one responds to their environment.

3. **Stress Behaviors:** highlights behaviors that emerge when an individual's needs are not met or when they are under stress. These stress behaviors, which can be counterproductive, offer insight into what may be causing discomfort or dissatisfaction.

4. **Interests:** also assesses individual interests, which reveal the types of work, projects, or activities that naturally engage a person, providing direction for career planning and development.

Each of these assessments can bring a different opportunity for your personal growth, making them useful in various contexts depending on where you are in your career and your personal development.

Other books I would highly recommend for your personal growth are: 1. "The Pathfinder: How to Choose or Change Your Career for a Lifetime of Satisfaction and Success" (Nicholas Lore, 2011), 2. "Now, Discover your Strengths" (Buckingham and Clifton, 2001) and 3. "From Strength to Strength" (Arthur C. Brooks, 2022).

Essential Learning Points

1. Investing in personalized professional development, whether it's a personality assessment or an assessment that measures your natural abilities, interests, or value, are all great resources that can help you grow.

2. There are several resources available for your personal development, including the Highlands Ability Battery, Myers-Briggs Type Indicator, True Colors Test, Five Voices Assessment, and The Birkman Method.

3. These resources can also be used to develop cohesion and trust amongst a team.

4. Using various personalized assessments will enhance your self-awareness, improve your interpersonal communication, and remind you of "why" you are a teacher. It will help you reflect on how valuable you are to the teaching profession and lead you to a path of joy!

Testimony

"Having administered the Highlands Ability Battery since 1995, I've found that the objective, non-evaluative insights it provides resonate deeply with people, often uncovering the 'why' behind their gut-level self-awareness. Gaining the language and words to articulate your best self brings a new level of clarity—one that is truly liberating. And that clarity fosters personal and professional satisfaction, collaboration, and productivity.

Productivity at work has a ripple effect. When you're working productively, it energizes you and fuels other areas of your life. The opposite is also true—working unproductively can be draining, leaving little energy for anything else. No job perfectly aligns with all of your natural talents and the skills you develop, so there are always decisions to make: Which aspects of your job feel required, and which can you supplement outside of work?

Sometimes, productivity isn't just about abilities and skills—it's also about your interests, values, goals, and career stage. The way these factors come together at any given moment determines how productive you feel, and this dynamic shifts over time. Using a guiding framework, such as the Whole Person Model, helps navigate these changes while reinforcing the perspective that you're not alone."

— Dori Stiles, Ph.D., Turning Points Coaching and Consulting

ACTIVITY 5

ACTIVITY 5A: Write a short narrative on what you would like your coworkers to know about you. Include what you would like to work with and how it is best to communicate with you. If you need assistance, some of the resources listed above have free online assessments. After you write your introduction, ask the people you are closest to (family or coworkers) to see if they would add anything.

_____
_____
_____
_____
_____

ACTIVITY 5B: Identify what is what is most important to you:

Values	Interests	Relationships
_____	_____	_____
_____	_____	_____
_____	_____	_____
_____	_____	_____
_____	_____	_____

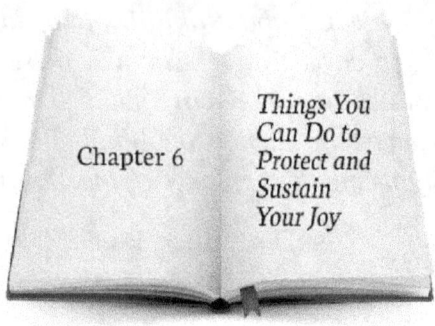

Chapter 6

Things You Can Do to Protect and Sustain Your Joy

"Let Joy be your journey – not in some distant goal."

– Tim Cook

Leslie was on her way back home to Atlanta from her mission trip in South Africa. She had just completed an incredible journey working with teachers at a private primary school. Over the past two weeks, she had cherished every moment with her family and the educators she had built relationships with over the past two years. As she settled into her seat for the 16-hour flight, she became emotional, reflecting on how much she loved the students and teachers in South Africa. She felt reassured that she was fulfilling her calling as an educator and was reminded of why she had entered the profession so many years ago.

However, midway through her flight over the Atlantic Ocean, her excitement slowly gave way to anxiety as she thought about returning to work on Monday morning. She had been able to take this trip over the Labor Day holiday, missing only eight days of school, but now the weight of her responsibilities loomed large. Her husband reassured her that she was simply exhausted from the trip, but Leslie felt otherwise.

She admitted to her husband that while her time in Africa had been refreshing, she was anxious about going back to work. She loved her students and teaching and knew she was in the right profession, but she was struggling to balance work with life outside the classroom. She felt that the challenges at school were impacting her attitude in the evenings and on weekends. The mission trip had been the first thing all year that didn't feel like work. She realized her life was out of balance and worried that she wasn't being the best wife—or the best mom to her pups.

Determined to make a change, Leslie and her husband decided to use the remaining eight hours of their flight to create a plan of action. Their goal was not just to help her survive work but to protect the fire and positive spirit she had felt when she first boarded the plane in Johannesburg.

Before developing solutions, Leslie needed to understand what was causing her the most stress at work. She made a list:

1. The next school break was still more than two months away.

2. Her principal's observation was coming up in two weeks.

3. She had a new student who spoke very little English. Spanish was spoken at home, and he was struggling academically and emotionally, which deeply concerned her.

4. She felt isolated from her grade-level team because her classroom was far from the other first-grade teachers.

Before landing in Atlanta, Leslie outlined some action steps to help her regain balance and joy.

First, she committed to getting a good night's sleep and starting each morning with a cup of coffee and an intentional, big smile—even if she had to fake it. Normally, she woke up happy, but on the tough mornings, she would act happy until she felt happy.

She also identified specific things at work she could control to reduce stress:

1. **Letting go of anxiety about her principal's observation.** Her principal had hired her five years ago and had always given her excellent ratings. She was always well-prepared for her lessons, so this was not something to stress over.

2. **Seeking help from the school counselor for her new student.** She was committed to supporting him by building a stronger relationship with his parents and researching resources to help his family adjust to the school culture. Instead of seeing this as a challenge, she would reframe it as an opportunity.

3. **Engaging more with her grade-level team.** She would arrive at school five minutes earlier each morning to walk down their hall and say good morning. Additionally, she would make an effort to eat lunch with them three days a week instead of sitting alone in her classroom.

4. **Planning another mission trip to South Africa next year—and inviting colleagues.** This would give her something exciting to look forward to.

As Leslie reflected on her growing anxiety, she realized how much her job was draining her and affecting her home life. By the time she got home from work, she was so exhausted that she barely had the energy to give her husband and pups the attention they needed. She asked her husband to help her come up with strategies for improving her work-life balance. She knew she couldn't completely turn off the emotions and energy from work, but she could learn to manage them better.

Together, they came up with a few commitments to help her feel more present and fulfilled at home:

1. Taking longer walks with her pups in the morning and after dinner to stay connected and get more exercise.

2. Establishing **Friday night date nights**—going out to dinner with her husband and sometimes bringing their pups.

3. Listening to **inspirational podcasts** during her 25-minute commute to work and for five minutes before bedtime.

4. Stopping all work-related emails and school tasks by 6:00 p.m.—and not checking emails before bed.

By the time the plane landed, Leslie felt more hopeful. She knew she couldn't change everything overnight, but with a clear plan, she could take meaningful steps toward regaining balance and joy—both at work and at home.

Leslie was concerned about returning to a life where maintaining a healthy work/life balance was a constant challenge. The reality of her situation reflects a common struggle. There are times when life feels out of balance, when the workload of being a teacher becomes overwhelming and starts to impact personal well-being, or when the demands of home and work pull us in multiple directions. It's essential to recognize that work/life balance isn't about completely separating work from home; rather, it's about understanding how to protect best the values, interests, and relationships that matter most.

I define work/life balance as:

"The ability to balance your energy and emotions between your teaching responsibilities and personal life in a way that promotes overall well-being, health, and satisfaction while safeguarding your values, interests, and relationships."

There are three fundamental principles to achieving work/life balance:

1. **Prioritize energy and emotions over time when defining work/life balance.** Using time as a measurement for balance can be misleading because time is a variable that shifts. For example, summer vacation allows for more family time, while a busy school event like Homecoming Week might involve evening or weekend commitments. A nighttime parent orientation inevitably takes away from family time. Instead of focusing solely on hours, it's more effective to manage the energy and emotions invested in both work and personal life.

2. **Acknowledge that energy and emotion from work and personal life overlap.** In reality, professional and personal lives are not entirely separate. The emotions and energy from work often follow us home, as Leslie experienced. Likewise, exhaustion or stress at work—like John in the previous chapter—can cause personal challenges. Unlike the fictional world of Severance, where employees Mark S. and Helly R. undergo a procedure that completely separates their work and personal lives, we cannot compartmentalize our experiences so neatly. In that series, memory access is dictated by location, creating two entirely separate lives—one at work and one at home. But in our reality, work and home life inevitably impact each other. The key is finding a way to support both.

3. **Define your ideal work/life balance:** Clarifying what balance looks like for you will help identify the values, interests, and relationships that should take priority. Once you establish these priorities and ensure they are protected, you can safeguard your path to joy and prevent burnout—both personally and professionally. The ultimate goal is to cultivate a positive mindset, sustain joy in the classroom, and maintain fulfillment at home.

I will first share my own priorities. Then, I will outline how you can protect yours by creating a Personal Vision Statement and implementing 15 actionable strategies to instantly enhance work/life balance and protect your path to joy in both your classroom and home life!

My Priorities

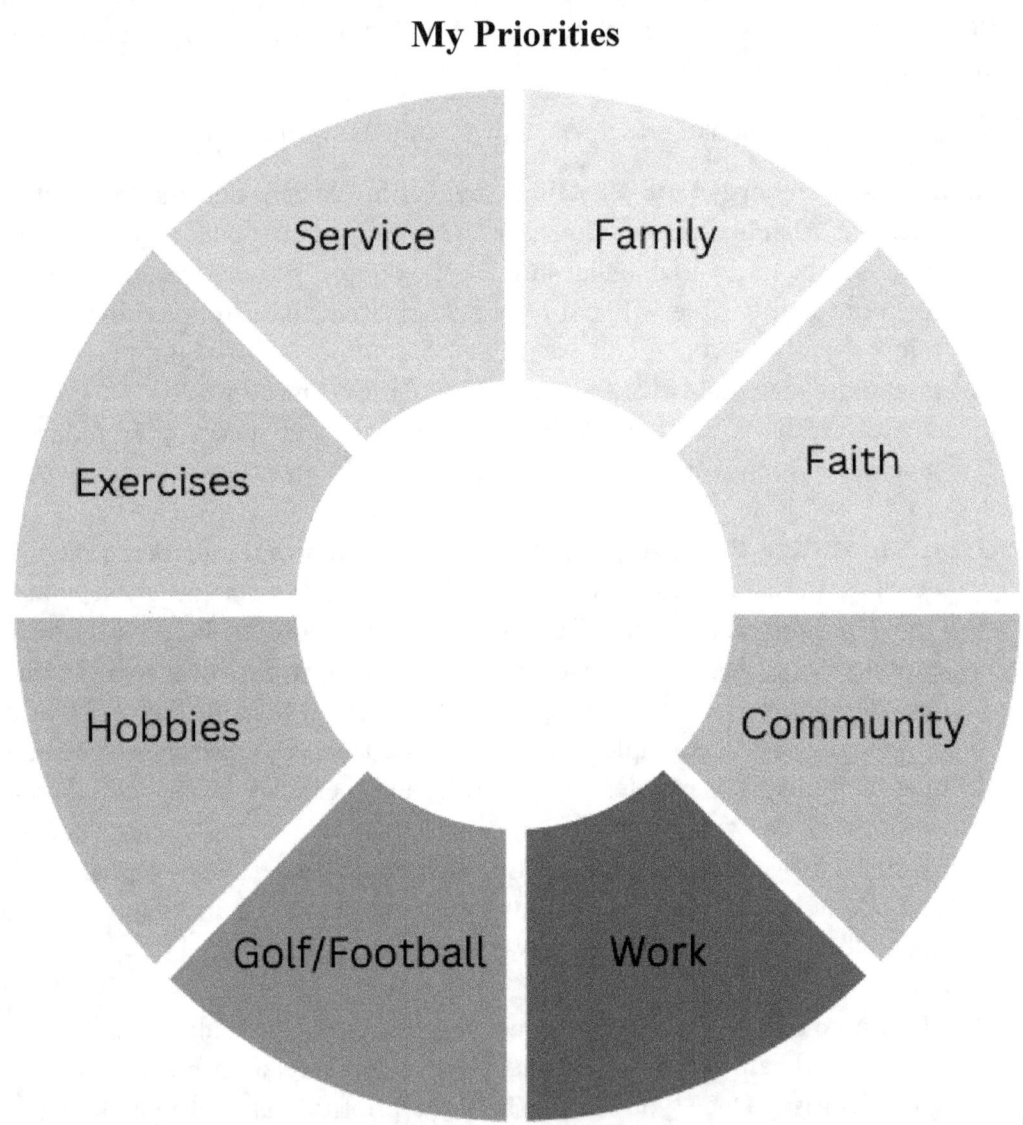

In Chapter 4, Focus on the <u>Things You Can Control</u>, I listed several things that were within your control at work, and here I've listed things you can do that will enhance your joy and sustain it in your daily life, personally and professionally. This information is some of the most important advice in this book on how to live a joyful life.

One of the most important things you can do to establish and protect what is most important to you and protect your path to joy is to create a Personal Vision Statement.

"A Personal Vision Statement is a unique expression of what is most important to you and serves as a guide for how you want to conduct your life. It is a living document that is fluid and can be changed as the person writing it changes. Once crafted, a Personal Vision Statement should be reviewed regularly and modified periodically." (Dr. Dori Stiles, Turning Points Coaching and Consulting, 2015)

Here is my Personal Vision Statement:

My Personal Vision is to positively impact the lives of others by:

- Serving as a loving and faithful husband and a loving and encouraging father,
- Committing to staying strong in my faith,
- Modeling a healthy lifestyle by exercising daily and eating healthy,
- Smiling every day, even on the rainy days,
- Having a positive mindset and seeing the good in everyone and an opportunity in every situation,
- Encouraging others and providing guidance when needed,
- Displaying honesty and integrity,
- Creating situations that are win/win,
- Celebrating successes, results, and progress, even the small ones,
- And being a compassionate and empathetic leader.

A Personal Vision Statement is an important tool that gets your values, interests, and relationships on paper and can be a great aide to help you be intentional on protecting your priorities and achieving your idea of work/life balance. My Personal Vision Statement enabled me to reflect on what my priorities were and to align my professional career path with my personal life. It gave me a greater sense of life satisfaction that I was in the right career as an educator.

"People who develop and monitor their Personal Vision Statement often describe themselves as living a balanced life. They are typically more satisfied, more productive, and experience more meaning and enjoyment in their jobs. Whereas people who do not have a Personal Vision Statement are more driven by wealth and power, and are reactive in their decision-making. They often describe themselves as living a stressful life and typically experience symptoms of stress and or burnout." (Dr. Dori Stiles, Turning Points Coaching and Consulting, 2015)

In addition to a Personal Vision Statement, I came up with 15 other things that you can do in your daily/weekly lives to help you live a life of joy at work and home.

1. **Make Attitude Your Personality**		Wave hello to your neighbors and smile everywhere you go. Ask the servers in a restaurant if they're having a nice day, leave bottles of water on your front porch for the Amazon driver, and carry a case of water in your backseat for a homeless person asking for help when you are stopped at a light. Being positive is something you can do even when you don't feel like it. The old saying is, "Fake it until you make it." You will be surprised how contagious being positive can be. When you pay it forward at Chick-fil-a, chances are they will pay it forward for the person behind them.

2. Your Prayer Life		Having a prayer life can be a source of comfort, inspiration, and personal growth, enhancing your connection to yourself, others, and your faith. Prayer can reduce anxiety and stress and create a safe space for peace, calmness, and stillness amidst the challenges of teaching and life. Prayer can encourage introspection and help you reflect on your actions, your emotions, and the things you are most grateful for. Engaging in prayer with others or attending a church will foster a sense of community and shared purpose with people who share similar beliefs.
3. Focus On Your Breathing	Exhale ↑ Inhale → ↓ ← Inhale	Focused breathing can alleviate some of your stress. I learned that, like most people, I get tense in stressful situations. In these situations, my breathing slows, my muscles tighten, and my blood pressure goes up. I know that I get tense when someone cuts me off or refuses to use a turn signal. I also notice I get a little unnerved every time someone leaves their shopping cart in the middle of the parking lot! I am sure there are things in your life that simply just bother you and cause frustration. Like some of you, I think I might have control issues because what stresses me out is the fact that I don't have control over these things. I can't make everyone put the shopping cart in the bay where they belong. But I do have control of how I respond and how many carts I push back to the cart corral.
		I learned a breathing technique from one of my counselors (thank you, Stefanie) that has been extremely helpful in lessening my stress when driving, watching the Eagles, and even when I'm sitting in the dentist's chair. Simply follow the arrows on the rectangle diagram and go slow. I've used this strategy to

		manage pain and anxiety. The strategy involves controlling your breathing, which in turn gets more oxygen to your brain. This causes your mind to help calm your body down. It's as simple as finding a rectangle. You'll notice that the world is full of rectangles. "You will continue to suffer if you have an emotional reaction to everything that is said to you. True power is sitting back and observing everything with logic. If words control you that means everyone else can control you. Breathe and allow things to pass." Bruce Lee
4. **Daily Journaling/ Meditation**		Daily journaling allows you to get things off your mind and onto paper or your computer. It can help you clear your mind and foster mental clarity, emotional well-being, and personal growth. Journaling and meditation allow you to reflect on your thoughts and feelings and allow you to slow your breathing while reducing your stress. Journaling and meditation allow you the opportunity to focus more on positive experiences and achievements, which will promote a more positive outlook. Taking time in a peaceful, quiet setting helps you reset your mind and help you gain a deeper understanding of yourself.
5. **Build Your Confidence**		"Confidence can be your SUPERPOWER. You need to look confident even when you're not." (Unknown) Confidence is something you can build through experience and practice. Public speaking is one of our top fears and the best way to get better at public speaking is to do it. Don't be afraid to try something new, whether it's a new activity with your class or you take on a new hobby, like pickleball. Trying a new activity in the classroom that fails is not failure. It is an incredible learning opportunity, and trying a new hobby can be fun, even if you're not that good at first. I got nervous when my kids signed me up for a cycling class, where you ride a stationary bike to a video and an instructor who is super hyped with enthusiasm. I was the oldest one

		in the class and the most out of shape. While my kids poked fun at me after the first three minutes, I convinced myself that I would probably never see these people ever again, and I was there to get a workout. I had to have confidence that all I needed to care about was my own workout and surviving this new experience, and the time with my kids, even if they made fun of me. Doing things that make you uncomfortable helps build confidence. The hardest golf shot is when you're standing at the first tee, and 20 other golfers are watching you. I used to be so worried about embarrassing myself but the more opportunities I had to tee off in front of an audience, the more confident I got. And after spending time watching the golfers in front of me, I learned that they weren't that good either. Try not to care so much what people think about you, even if you hit a bad shot. Focus on the next shot and not what others think.
6. **Choose Your Friends Wisely**		I try to always surround myself with people who are more positive than I am and who consistently lift me up. After I read John Gordon's "Energy Bus," I quickly learned to avoid energy vampires. Look for people who can mentor you and people you can mentor. Find groups of people that share your values and interests, whether it's a book club, small group, or softball team. You can also join an art or dance class, attend community events, and join a gym rather than working out at home. Personality matches are super important, so shy away from people who drag you down, the "energy vampires." Everyone is not for you, and you are not for everyone. That is perfectly ok! "You become who you hang around with." (Dave Ramsey)
7. **Make Good Choices**		This sounds so simple, but I would bet you probably make hundreds of decisions every day. Realize how much you control your own life and the choices you make. You choose what you are wearing to work, your breakfast, and what you will listen to on your way to school. In addition, you make the

		choices on how you will spend your money and other difficult decisions. Whenever I am faced with making a difficult choice, I always ask myself two questions: • What is the good I seek to achieve? and • What are the intended and unintended consequences of my decision? The choices I own, and I also own the consequences. I always try to make sure I have all the information I can get before I make my decision, whether it's buying a car or deciding what I'm wearing to school. When I make the decision, I own it! No matter how big or small.
8. **Sleep Habits Matter**		Getting the right amount of sleep each night is essential for your physical and mental health. The Mayo Clinic, a not-for-profit medical group practice, recommends that adults should get at least 7 hours of sleep each night. Less than that, on a consistent basis, can lead to health issues. In addition, it is confirmed by many psychologists, that the 30 minutes prior to going to sleep can play a critical role in your sleep patterns. Dr. Robin Haight, a clinical psychologist, believes that you should avoid intense conversations, scary movies, and sending last-minute texts just before bedtime. Your brain needs the downtime to get a good night's sleep. Please don't check your work email right before going to sleep. It's never a good idea!
9. **Your Hobbies**		Do things that are fun and make you feel good. Whether it's golfing, reading a book, playing pickleball, or taking long walks with your pup or pups! Do things that energize you and make you feel good. Playing golf is more than trying to get a good scorecard. It allows me to be with good friends and family, get exercise, and enjoy nature. It also allows me to get some exercise. Find activities that get you outside!

10. Take Care of Your Health		These items are not in rank order, and if they were, this would be at the top. If you don't have your health, you will be severely limited in what you can do. A balanced diet provides the body with the nutrients it needs to function optimally, supporting energy levels and mental wellness. Regular exercise strengthens the heart, improves circulation, and boosts physical fitness. Exercise also relieves stress and promotes mental wellness. Make sure you see your doctor regularly to get your blood pressure and other vitals checked. Your doctor can help provide guidance on your nutrition and level of exercise.
11. Celebrate Your Successes and Progress		Make birthdays, anniversaries, and every Friday a big deal to celebrate. Remember, joy is not just the end goal; be intentional about having joy by celebrating even the smallest things, like when a new recipe is a big hit! If your goal is to run two miles, don't wait until you hit the two-mile mark to celebrate. Celebrate each step you take to reach your goal. This is the same thing with your children. Teach them to celebrate their progress and results and celebrate with them.
12. Watch Movies, Have a 'Go To' Playlist, Listen To Podcasts, and Read Books that Inspire You		I hear all the time that we need to put down our technology and limit our screen time. In my personal life, I was more concerned with how I was using my technology vs the number of hours of screen time. Isn't it nice that our iPhones remind us how much time we spend on them? I use technology for inspirational videos and I have my favorite movie watchlist that I pull out whenever I need a lift. I enjoy reading books and listening to podcasts that inspire me or challenge me to become a better leader.

My Movie Playlist

    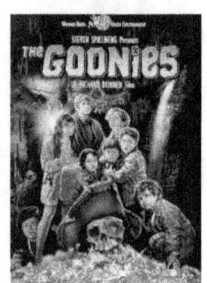

In addition to movies, there are songs that inspire me when I exercise, when I drive, and even when I play golf. Here is my "Happy Playlist":

Nothings Gonna Stop Us Now by Starship	Don't Stop Me Now by Queen
Mr. Blue Sky by ELO	End of the Line by The Traveling Wilburys
Three Little Birds by Bob Marley	I Won't Back Down by Tom Petty
Lease on Life by Andy Grammer	We Are The World by USA for Africa
Don't Stop Believing by Journey	St. Elmo's Fire by John Parr

Here are some of my favorite books:

13. Take Time for Service		Helping others and giving back can bring you satisfaction and the experience of helping the less fortunate. Volunteering, mentoring, and offering extra support to those in need can be very fulfilling. Volunteering also puts you around people who have a servant's heart. If your school or community provides service opportunities, it is a great thing to build your joy and be a part of a loving community.
14. Protect Downtime		This is an area that may sound insignificant, but with today's reliance on technology, we are connected to people and information more than ever before. The challenge is we don't often give our brains a chance to unwind. Downtime is needed and healthy. It can increase energy by resetting the brain and helps us regain our emotional focus. Put your technology down and do activities like go for a walk, go to the driving range, or do a 2,000-piece puzzle. Doing things that can take your mind off work and the busyness of the world. You have my permission to give yourself a break, and you don't have to feel guilty if you find yourself taking a nap.
15. Be Kind to Yourself		A lot of times, we are the most critical of ourselves! If a lesson bombs, or you're five minutes late to work, cut yourself a break! Every failure is a learning opportunity, and sometimes, things happen that are out of our control, like getting a flat tire and being late to work. Many of us are our own worst critics, and we often find it easier to show others grace for their mistakes. We tend to beat ourselves up when we don't meet our own expectations, whether it's a lesson that doesn't go well or our students do poorly on an exam. Remember that each opportunity is a learning opportunity, and be kind to yourself. We are all far from perfect.

All of these things can be utilized daily, weekly, monthly, or whenever needed. If you are feeling stressed at work, identify your top three strategies and lean on them! For me, it's a round of golf, listening to my Happy Song List, or watching one of my movies. But my number one "go-to" is taking my pups for a walk. If you are finding having a work-life balance and you are constantly stressed, go back to your family values and identify what is most important to you. Is it spending time with family, being active, or going to church? Sometimes, you will lessen your stress simply by putting yourself in a safe environment or with safe people.

"Showing up is 90% of the solution."

– Woody Allen

Taking care of yourself takes practice, but it's the best investment you can make for your emotional and mental health. Don't ever feel guilty for taking time for yourself. Being intentional about your own well-being is critical for you to live a life of joy!

Essential Learning Points

1. It is critical for you to define what work/life balance means to you. Writing a Personal Vision Statement is a great tool to help you identify your values, interests, and relationships that are most important to you and what you should focus your energy and time on.

2. Identify three strategies that are your "go-to" when you are stressed or need a break. It can be a nice walk outside, a book, a movie, or hanging out with a friend. Identify the strategies that are best for you.

3. Don't ever feel guilty for taking the time to invest in your mental, emotional, and physical well-being.

4. Having strategies to protect your priorities and your well-being is critical to keeping your joy at work and at home.

Testimony

It can be difficult for teachers to balance work and home life and still feel the passion they once felt when they first started teaching. In the 23 years I have been a teacher, there have been many times that I have felt completely overwhelmed due to work responsibilities, personal responsibilities as well as a combination of both. I often found myself juggling multiple roles, balancing the demands of my profession with my personal life.

Over the years, I learned to make it a point to lean on a mix of passion, purpose, and self-care. Small victories in the classroom, moments of connection with students, and watching them succeed are what make all of the stress, preparation, and late nights worth it. It is extremely important to have a healthy balance of both work and personal life. I make it a priority to set clear boundaries, like limiting after-hours grading or planning and use time management strategies to stay organized to avoid having to prioritize my work over my family. I make sure to dedicate myself fully to spending quality time with my family attending my children's school events, sporting events, and other extra-curricular activities. Whether it's going out or just having a movie night, it is important to dedicate these irreplaceable moments to family, hobbies, and rest.

My oldest daughter is currently in college to become a High School History teacher, and I believe it has a lot to do with the amazing teachers that impacted her life, as well as her witnessing first-hand the joy teaching has brought to my life.

> – Karen Spurka, 23 years of experience
> teaching middle school Special
> Education and Finance Literacy

ACTIVITY 6

ACTIVITY 6A: Create your Personal Vision Statement incorporating the values, interests, and relationships that are important to you.

_____

_____

_____

ACTIVITY 6B: List three things you can do daily that will help sustain your joy.

_____

_____

_____

ACTIVITY 6C: List three goals you would like to accomplish over the next 3 months.

_____

_____

_____

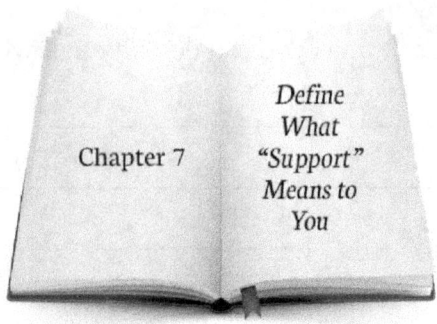

"Geese always support each other. When a goose gets injured, two birds accompany it down to the ground. Just as geese do, we must support each other."

– Emma Hayes

Ann and Bill are two teachers on the fourth-grade team at Hillside Primary School. Their team consists of six other teachers. Ann is in her third year at Hillside, while Bill has been at the school since it opened 18 years ago. Over the years, their team has become a model for collaboration. Every Monday after school, they meet with the curriculum director and principal to work on the school's strategic vision and professional development plan. At the beginning of the year, their team was recognized at a faculty meeting, where each member received a certificate of recognition and a gift card to the local market. Recently, Ann and Bill's team were invited to present at a conference in Oxford in July.

In her third year, Ann is thriving and feels valued as a teacher at Hillside. She takes it as a compliment that her principal and curriculum director dedicate time to her team. She sees herself as part of something special and appreciates the direct access she has to school leadership. Her principal frequently stops by her classroom to visit her and her students, making her feel supported and encouraged. Ann believes her principal is invested in her success and welcomes her feedback. When she was recognized in front of the entire faculty, she felt appreciated and loved—plus, the gift card provided a nice weekend meal. Ann is feeling great about her job, herself, and her relationship with her principal.

On the other hand, Bill's morale is not thriving under the same leadership. While he loves teaching, his students, and his colleagues, he is frustrated by the extra work he has taken on. Spending every Monday after school with his principal and curriculum director feels like a chore rather than a valuable use of his time. Bill would much rather be out hitting golf balls. Though he recognizes his experience and knowledge as valuable, and he is happy to mentor Ann and his teammates, he resents the administration. He believes they are using his team's success to promote their own agendas. When his principal stops by his classroom, Bill perceives it as scrutiny rather than support. He simply wants to be left alone to teach. He even found the faculty recognition at the beginning of the year frustrating, feeling that a market gift card was hardly fair compensation for the additional work. Bill is struggling; while he loves teaching, he does not feel supported by his principal or the school leadership.

Is it possible for a principal or school leader to create an environment where one teacher thrives while another feels frustrated? Absolutely. What motivates and makes us feel valued varies because we all have different needs, values, and interests. One of the leading causes of teacher burnout is the "lack of administrative support." However, before addressing the issue of support, we must clearly define what it means. Without a shared understanding of support, the issue may be difficult to resolve.

When teachers express, "My supervisor doesn't support me," they often struggle to articulate exactly what they mean. The reality is that when there is a significant gap between the support teachers need and the level of support they receive, frustration and burnout occur.

To help teachers avoid frustration, there needs to be an alignment between their expectations and the support they receive. In the example above, Bill does not appear to be receiving the support he expects, while Ann feels fully supported. It is crucial for both teachers to understand what support they need and communicate those expectations to their principal.

What can Bill do to reduce his frustration and improve his morale?

Bill decided to meet with his principal to share his concerns and expectations. When he requested a meeting, his principal was willing to meet on the same day. Bill appreciated her responsiveness and led the conversation by outlining the key issues causing his frustration, including the extra after-school meetings, frequent classroom visits, and mandatory summer training. He chose not to bring up the market gift card, not wanting to seem petty. His principal took notes and, in turn, shared her perspective, laying out what she considered non-negotiable. She appreciated Bill bringing his concerns to her attention and valued his honesty.

His principal explained that she expected him to remain an engaged and positive contributor to his team because he was one of her exemplary teachers. She shared that she frequently visited his classroom because she always learned something new from observing him. However, she acknowledged that she had never provided him with feedback after her visits and apologized for that oversight. Understanding his concerns, she proposed rotating the after-school meetings to alternate between Monday afternoons and a morning session that fit Bill's schedule. Additionally, she granted Bill the option to skip the summer conference if he had a scheduling conflict, though she encouraged him to attend, emphasizing its potential benefits. She thanked Bill for meeting with her and expressed appreciation for his dedication.

When Bill left the meeting, he felt heard and valued. He was pleased with the new meeting schedule and now understood why his principal frequently visited his class. As a 95% introvert, he had always felt uncomfortable being used as an example for other teachers, but he now recognized his principal's intentions. He did not want to disappoint her. Although he still disliked public recognition, he accepted it as part of the job and decided to handle it with a better mindset. Most importantly, he was relieved to have his summer back.

In this example, Bill's proactive approach to meeting with his principal allowed him to gain clarity on the level of support he needed and a better understanding of his principal's expectations. Before the meeting, Bill felt unsupported. However, after their discussion, his perspective shifted. His principal's willingness to meet with him immediately made him feel important, and her flexibility empowered him to make decisions about his involvement in the summer conference. While Bill still found the extra meetings challenging, he recognized their value to his team and principal.

Had Bill continued without addressing his frustrations, he would have remained discontented. Instead, by initiating the conversation, he gained clarity, reducing much of his frustration and allowing him to refocus on what he loves most: teaching.

The next action step in your path to joy is understanding the importance of taking ownership of what support looks like in your role as a teacher—and ensuring these expectations are clearly communicated to others. This doesn't guarantee that others will always meet your expectations, but it does help prevent unnecessary frustration caused by unspoken assumptions. Take Bill's situation, for example—his principal's frequent classroom visits frustrated him because he assumed they were meant to scrutinize him. However, by addressing his concerns directly, he gained clarity: either the visits would decrease, or he would receive feedback from them. In both scenarios, Bill's frustration was alleviated because he now understood that his principal wasn't out to get him. This clarity is crucial in your own journey to joy. By clearly defining the support you need to succeed in your job, you allow others the opportunity to meet your needs.

The next chapter, titled Managing Up, will provide additional guidance on how to advocate for the support you need to thrive in your teaching role—and what to do if that support isn't forthcoming.

I'd like to believe that every school leader has good intentions when it comes to supporting teachers, especially since most of them were once teachers themselves. If they weren't, they likely worked closely with teachers in other roles, such as counselors, school psychologists, or instructional coaches. Regardless of their background, a positive school culture is only possible when collaboration exists between teachers and leadership. Feeling supported is a critical factor in a teacher's success—it influences effectiveness, job satisfaction, and, ultimately, student learning outcomes. Teachers are the closest to students and families, making them the foundation of a school's culture.

While principals and school leaders play key roles in providing guidance and resources, I believe teachers are uniquely positioned to define the type of support they need to thrive. Teachers should have the authority to articulate what support looks like and how to sustain a productive, collaborative relationship with their principals and school leadership.

My goal is to help you identify the support you need and show you that you have more control over the level of support you receive than you might think. Because you work closest with students and parents, you have firsthand knowledge of what's happening within your school community. In a positive school culture, where teachers feel empowered and valued, there is a strong foundation of trust between teachers and administrators. For clarity, I'll refer to "principal" throughout this discussion, but this applies to any school leader serving in a supervisory role. When your expectations of leadership align with the support you receive, trust strengthens, and your confidence and effectiveness as an educator grow. And when you feel confident and capable in your work, joy follows.

Expectations SET = Expectations MET = Confidence/Effectiveness $\uparrow$ and JOY $\uparrow$

(Teacher)　　　　　(Leader)

Effective school leaders prioritize making their teachers feel valued. Strong principals recognize that a "one-size-fits-all" approach to resources and training is ineffective. Instead, they create a school environment that builds upon the diverse backgrounds, experiences, and skill sets of their teachers. A first-year teacher has vastly different needs than a twenty-year veteran, and effective leadership acknowledges and accommodates these differences.

When teachers feel valued and are granted a degree of autonomy, a culture emerges where they support one another both professionally and emotionally. This collaborative environment allows teachers to develop skills in one another that help meet the diverse needs of their students. Support should come from both peers and school leadership. Teachers should expect open lines of communication with their principal—both in terms of advocating for their needs and receiving consistent communication from leadership.

I have read hundreds of leadership books, and two of my favorites are The 7 Habits of Highly Effective People (Stephen R. Covey, 1989) and Leaders Eat Last (Simon Sinek, 2017). Both books highlight what effective leadership looks like and what strong leaders do. Over the years, I have worked under school leaders who helped me thrive and others who, to put it politely, showed me what not to do as a leader. While my school leaders changed, my expectations for the support I needed to succeed remained the same.

Below, I have outlined the support I expected from my principal to thrive. While I respected the different visions and personalities of the leaders I worked under, I never hesitated to challenge the level of support I was receiving or to question school processes. My vision for leadership was shaped during my years as a teacher, and without realizing it at the time, it ultimately became the foundation of my leadership style as a principal.

WHAT I EXPECTED FROM MY PRINCIPAL (ADMINISTRATOR)

To be kind and welcoming to me and my students.
To be accessible to meet with me if I have a question and respond to my emails
To be visible around the school and at school events
To protect my personal time by not sending emails after 4:00 on Fridays or on weekends
To have a vision for the school and communicate that vision
To include teachers in decision-making when appropriate and communicate decisions that are made by leadership
To be a coach and encourage teachers to grow
To handle parent issues at the lowest level and have my back
To celebrate school successes and progress-to be a cheerleader for the school.
To take an interest in knowing me personally- asking about my children would be an example (I'm not asking to be best friends or go out for Happy Hour)
To only have meetings when necessary if it can be communicated through email, no need to meet
To be honest and provide critical feedback and not fluff

The most effective principals and school leaders are those who genuinely invest in their teachers and make them feel valued. Just as our students come to us with unique learning styles, interests, and skill sets, so do our teachers. While school leaders cannot be everything to everyone, the most effective principals recognize and build upon the strengths of their teachers, understanding that teachers are the true culture builders of the school.

When teachers' expectations of support from administration are met, they can thrive both professionally and personally. However, when there is confusion or a lack of understanding about the level of support administrators can provide, frustration builds, leading to burnout and even causing teachers to seek employment elsewhere.

I want to empower you to help your supervisor understand your needs and what you require to be successful. You have the right to define the level of support you need—not just to survive in your role but to truly thrive. As a teacher, you are the backbone of your school, making the most significant daily impact on your students. Understanding and communicating your needs is a critical step in your journey toward joy and fulfillment in your profession.

My hope is that your supervisor is committed to providing the support you need to be successful, and I believe most leaders aspire to do just that. However, the next chapter will explore what you can do if your supervisor is unable to meet your expectations for success.

Essential Learning Points

1. A leader's leadership style can impact each teacher differently. It is important to understand that teachers have different definitions of what "support' means to them.

2. Frustration in the job leads to teacher burnout or teachers leaving their school. It is important for teachers to understand the support needed and communicate this with their supervisor. A positive relationship between a teacher and principal is critical to the culture of a school.

3. It is important for you to understand the support needed from people on your team, your grade level, and your administration. Expectations are crucial in building relationships with your peers and supervisors.

Testimony

As a lead teacher, I was willing and able to take on a variety of tasks. My administrator was impressed by my work ethic and encouraged me to seek Leadership Certification. I pursued this certification and received tremendous support and encouragement from my principal. I needed a mentor during my leadership internship and my principal agreed to take this role. He permitted me to be involved in many activities and situations, which provided me with great insight into the myriad of situations in leadership places one. I was often challenged by my principal to describe how I would handle a given situation, and then we would discuss the pros and cons of the decision I had made. He often provided constructive criticism, which allowed me to analyze my own decisions and grow as a professional.

The encouragement to pursue leadership certification and the support and feedback provided during my internship provided me with valuable learning tools. I felt valued and received the support I needed in my career as an educator.

- Cindy S. Boulware, 33 years of experience teaching Gifted/Social Sciences

ACTIVITY 7

ACTIVITY 7A: What does "support" mean to you? List the behaviors you expect from your principal that will make you feel supported:

_____

_____

_____

_____

_____

ACTIVITY 7B: You are in an interview and the principal asks you, "What support will you need to be successful teaching at our school?" How do you respond to this question?

_____

_____

_____

_____

_____

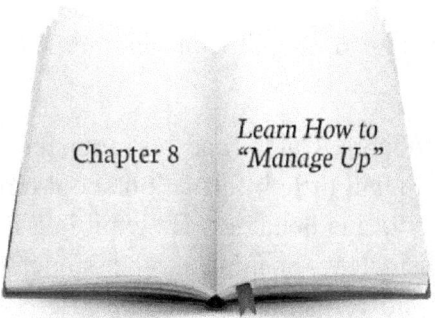

"Principals should strive to support their teachers by investing in their professional growth and emotional well-being. After all, teachers have the biggest and most direct impact on the students and in developing a positive school culture. Education is a people business, and the teachers are the foundation."

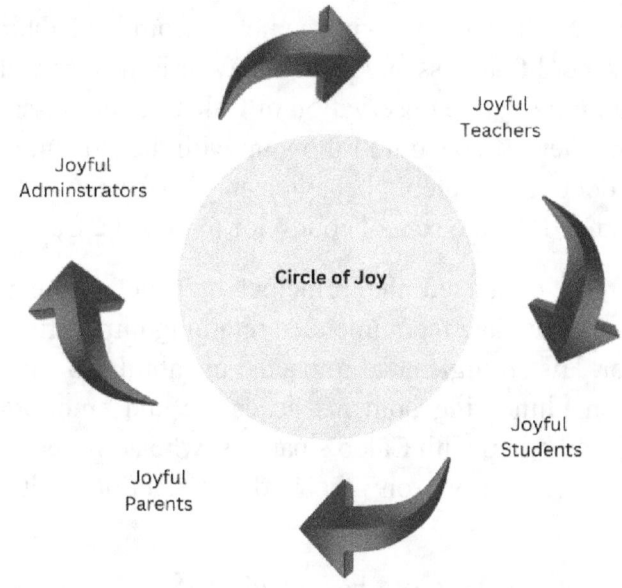

"THE CIRCLE OF JOY"

"Joyful Teachers make Joyful Students, Joyful Students make Joyful Parents, and Joyful Parents make Joyful Administrators."

Reagan is a second-grade teacher eager to begin her fifth school year. She has built a strong reputation and is beloved by both her students and her fellow teachers. As the school year approached, Reagan was particularly excited about the arrival of a new principal. The principal who had hired her retired over the summer, and the district promoted an assistant principal from another school within the district to take the role.

One of Reagan's new students, Caleb, had just transferred from a school on the other side of town. Reagan had little information about him, but from the first day, she became concerned about his behavior. He exhibited inappropriate interactions with both her and his classmates—pushing another student in line, grabbing French fries off a peer's plate, and refusing to sit down after being redirected multiple times. While Reagan understood that adjusting to a new school could be challenging, she also knew how crucial it was for students to start the year on the right foot.

After two days, Reagan's concerns deepened. She decided to share them with her new principal, Mrs. Joyce. During their meeting, Mrs. Joyce was welcoming and seemed genuinely invested in Reagan's concerns. Reagan clearly communicated the support she needed, including having someone from leadership follow up with Caleb's previous school to assess any prior behavior issues, as well as considering an evaluation or administrative observation of Caleb in her classroom. Mrs. Joyce assured Reagan that her office would follow up with the student's previous school and asked her to document Caleb's behavior and performance over the next few days. She also arranged for the school counselor to observe Caleb the next day.

Mrs. Joyce promptly contacted the principal at Caleb's previous school and discovered that the school had recommended retaining him in first grade due to his immature behavior. His struggles had impacted his ability to succeed in a general education classroom, hindering both his academic and emotional development. Mrs. Joyce then followed up with Caleb's parents, who admitted that their decision to transfer him was based on their dissatisfaction with the retention recommendation.

Understanding the complexity of the situation, Mrs. Joyce visited Reagan's classroom to inform her that a meeting had been scheduled for Friday morning. This meeting would include Reagan, the school counselor, and the director of student testing. She reassured Reagan that the team would work together to create a plan that prioritized both Caleb's needs and the well-being of the class.

In this situation, Reagan effectively communicated her concerns and the support she required. Mrs. Joyce responded swiftly and decisively—contacting the student's former school and parents, arranging for observation, and assembling the necessary personnel to address the issue. As a result, Reagan felt confident about the upcoming school year and reassured by the new leadership. She knew she had the support she needed to ensure both her and her students' success.

Stories like this highlight the invaluable partnerships between teachers and administrators in fostering a thriving learning environment. However, the unfortunate reality is that many teachers do not receive the support they need from their administrators. The lack of administrative support has become a significant factor in teacher dissatisfaction and attrition.

The UNESCO Global Teacher Report on Teachers: "Addressing Teacher Shortages and Transforming the Profession" (2024) highlights an urgent need for 44 million primary and secondary teachers worldwide by 2030. The report identifies a lack of support as a key factor pushing educators out of the profession. Similarly, a study by McKinsey & Company, which surveyed over 1,800 educators between February and May 2022, found that 31% cited poor leadership as a reason for leaving teaching. Additionally, the Workforce Survey conducted by the Professional Association of Georgia Educators (PAGE) in May 2024 revealed that 74% of teachers felt unsupported by their administrators.

Have you ever experienced a time when you felt unsupported by your administration or supervisor? How did you handle it? What do you do when you face challenges with a student or a parent and feel your administration is not offering adequate support? When administrators fail to support their staff, it can create tension, lower morale, and ultimately impact student success. The lack of administrative support is not only a leading cause of teachers leaving the profession but also the number one reason educators transfer schools.

Building positive relationships with school leaders can be challenging, but it is never insurmountable.

> *"Every relationship offers one of two things: a lesson or a blessing.*
> *In many instances, the lesson is the ultimate blessing."*

> — Anquanette Gaspard.

When an administrator is supportive, teacher morale increases, and both students and teachers can thrive in a positive school culture. A strong relationship between a teacher and their principal is crucial to fostering a productive school environment and achieving positive student outcomes.

While school administrators hold positions of authority, building a successful partnership requires the cooperation of both the administrator and the teacher. For clarity, I will use the term "administrator," which can refer to a principal, lead teacher, director, or similar role.

I believe there are two natural tendencies for both administrators and teachers that set the stage for a positive relationship:

1. Most school administrators can empathize with the needs of teachers since many of them were once teachers themselves. Teachers are often called to the profession, and administrators, having once been teachers, likely felt that same calling. Furthermore, administrators would not have advanced into leadership roles without the guidance and support of their own supervising school administrators. They should recognize how critical administrative support was to their growth as teachers.

2. While most teachers have never been administrators, they have spent thousands of hours in coursework and training to understand the support necessary for their success. When answering their calling to become teachers, they enter the profession excited and motivated to meet the needs of their students—all of them. They step into the field prepared for a partnership with their administrator.

In the last chapter, I discussed the importance of defining what "support" means to you and effectively communicating the support you need to your administrator. In this chapter, my goal is to expand on the support you require and share strategies for building positive relationships with your administrator while protecting your emotional well-being and maintaining your joy. While I believe most school administrators are committed to their teachers' success, the reality is that administrators sometimes make decisions—or fail to make decisions—that leave teachers feeling unsupported. However, I believe that whether or not you currently feel supported by your administrator, you can take proactive steps to secure the support you need.

The term I use to help teachers navigate their relationship with administrators is "Managing Up."

"Managing Up is a teacher's responsibility to engage in the educational process by building a positive partnership with their administrator. A trusting partnership between teacher and administrator is necessary to ensure teachers receive the support they need to perform their jobs to the best of their ability. Likewise, administrators must feel that they are effectively supporting the teachers under their supervision. This partnership fosters emotional safety for both parties, helping them resolve conflicts and address problems that arise. While administrators hold positional authority, a teacher's influence within this partnership should not be underestimated."

There are three critical components to "Managing Up":

- First, the lack of support may not be intentional. An administrator's inability to provide support may be due to factors beyond their control.

- Second, teachers should reflect on the level of authority they have within their role and focus on the aspects they can control.

- Third, teachers should use effective strategies to build a positive relationship with their administrator, ensuring their emotional well-being and preserving their sense of joy.

The ultimate goal is to cultivate and maintain a positive relationship in which both teachers and administrators feel respected and supported.

Part 1 of "Managing Up": your principal's inability to show you support may be due to factors outside his/her control.

They learn in graduate school that student performance outcomes improve when a school has highly qualified and passionate teachers, and an administrator's responsibility is to support the teachers who educate their students. I have never met an administrator who didn't want his or her teachers and students to be successful. However, even when an administrator has good intentions to support their teachers, there may be factors that limit their ability to provide the necessary support.

In Reagan's situation, if her principal had been unable to arrange for the counselor to observe her student, Reagan might have felt unsupported. If the counselor had been unavailable during the first two weeks of school, the principal may have lacked the immediate resources to address Reagan's concerns. At times, I have been guilty of feeling frustrated with my principal for not supporting me, only to later discover that external factors limited their ability to provide the support I requested. In retrospect, this frustration was a waste of emotional energy. Understanding the constraints that limited my principal's ability to support me helped put things in perspective and allowed me to maintain trust in my leader.

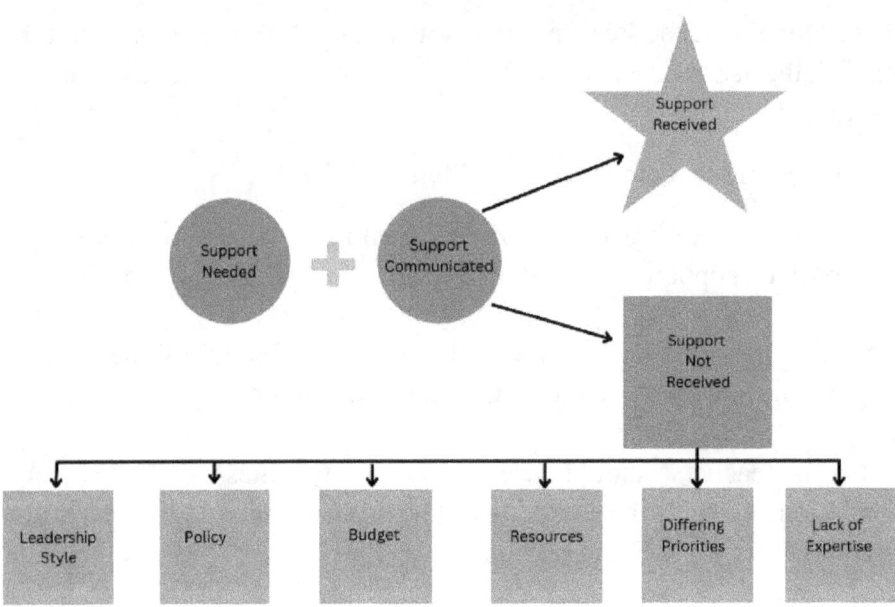

LEADERSHIP STYLE: *Just as teachers have different teaching styles and students have different learning styles, principals all have different leadership styles. School administrators are all born with unique strengths, abilities, and interests. It is possible that a teacher might not feel supported by the administrator simply because of his or her leadership style. I once interviewed a teacher who left her school because her principal didn't know her name. It is possible the principal could have been more of an introvert and preferred to delegate the authority of leading the teachers to his department heads. In addition, if a school has 130 teachers, it may be difficult for the principal to get to know all the teachers on a personal level. If the teacher wanted more personal investment from the principal, it is easy to see how the teacher might not feel supported.*

The way administrators communicate with teachers, their level of visibility, and if they are more top-down leaders or value teacher feedback, are just some examples of how an administrator demonstrates his or her leadership style. Some teachers may have trouble building a positive relationship with their principal if they have differing values or interests. A principal who loves football and attends every football game and talks football with the head football coach during lunch, may be perceived that he doesn't support the band.

Policy: *Every school and school system has policies in place that are designed to protect the integrity and operation of the school. In many cases policies are developed by local, state, or national government agencies. In some instances, a teacher may find a policy, or a school process causes frustration because it inhibits his or her ability to perform the job. Some schools have policies in place that all teachers must sign in and out each day. While the policy is in place for safety reasons, some teachers may see it as being micromanaged and a lack of trust for teachers.*

The good thing about policies and processes is they are time bound and do have the ability to be changed. A positive partnership between teachers and their administration can lead to a change or a creation of a new policy or process.

Budget: *All schools operate within a budget and the funding typically comes from governmental taxes, tuition fees, or fund raising. Typically, personnel costs are a significant percentage of the operating budget, and the remaining budget is used for maintenance and expenses to operate the school, including textbooks, technology, and buses. Schools generally are challenged to find new funding sources or reallocate funds to pay for new programs and initiatives. Sometimes teachers who cannot get funding from their principal for a classroom library, can apply for grants or donations to build it.*

Resources: *Resources include funding, personnel, facilities, buses, and any tool or piece of equipment that is necessary to operate the school. In Reagan's example, her principal was able to reallocate the counselor to observe her student. In some cases, a principal may not have the resources to allocate to observe or test a child the next day. Other examples include schools with increased enrollment have witnessed large class sizes because of the lack of resources, and many schools have struggled with the resources to provide on-line learning for students.*

Differing Priorities: _This occurs when a teacher, or teachers, and their administrator have different ideas on how to allocate the school's funds, resources, or time. Principals must answer to many stakeholders including teachers, parents, their superintendent, or supervisor, and even board members. Administrators can be under pressure to meet the needs of many stakeholders and teachers are often unaware of what these needs may be. Sometimes administrators are given directives by their supervisor that teachers would not be aware._

Lack of Expertise: _In addition to leadership style, administrators have different experiences, knowledge, and skillsets. This is not meant to be a criticism of administrators; running a school is very complex, and It is not realistic to expect an administrator to be an expert in every aspect of leading and operating a school. A principal who gains experience and is intentional on developing his/her knowledge and skills, will be much more effective in the role. In my first-year transitioning to administration, a veteran principal advised me that Principals in:_

> _Year 1: don't know what the issues are, and don't know how to solve them._
> _Year 2: begin to know what the issues are but still don't know how to solve them._
> _Year 3: now know what the issues are and now know how to solve them._

*A successful administrator understands that he/she will never have all the answers but can become experts on how to find the answers.

My hope is that by having a better understanding of the factors that can limit the amount of support from your principal, you will be able to differentiate whether the perceived lack of support is coming directly from your principal or a factor outside his or her authority or control. While it is important for a principal to empathize with his/her teachers, it can be equally important for teachers to empathize with the role of a principal in leading a school.

Part 2 of "Managing Up": you should reflect on the level of authority you have as a teacher and focus on the things within your control.

If you find yourself in a situation where you do not feel supported, understanding why you are or are not receiving the support you need is important in helping you navigate your relationship with your administrator. As a teacher, you have the authority to "manage up," and you are in control of how you respond to your administrator, whether you perceive that your principal is the reason for the lack of support or not. Here are some reminders of the things you are in control of in your relationship with your principal:

Support	How you define it and communicate it to your principal
Your Response	How you respond to your principal when you understand why you are not receiving support.
Your Attitude	Keeping your positive mindset that your principal is invested in your success
Your Timeline	Your sense of urgency or timeline when you need your concerns addressed
Your Documentation	It's important to take notes and keep your thoughts and facts organized.
Your Vulnerability	Determine how invested you are in your relationship with your principal.
Your Level of Engagement in Your School	Determine how much time and energy you are willing to spend on school committees and school-sponsored activities.
Your Strategies	The strategies you choose to build a positive relationship with your principal

You are in control of the strategies you choose to "manage up" with your administrator. Next, I want to share the 11 best practices I've experienced that can help you in your efforts to "manage up" and build a positive relationship with your principal. Remember, the goal is to create a positive partnership that will help you sustain your path to a joyful career.

Part 3 of "Managing Up": Strategies to build trust with your principal and protect your emotional well-being and your path to joy.

Maintain Professionalism at All Times	Professionalism is critical when working with your administrator. You should focus on your responsibilities, always remain calm under pressure, and avoid engaging in negative talk with other teachers about your administrator. Maintaining a high standard of professionalism sets a positive example for your colleagues and demonstrates a commitment to the school's mission. Challenge the policy or procedure but be careful challenging the person.
Engage Your Principal	This includes taking the lead on building a positive relationship with your administrator. Some things you can do include inviting your principal to visit your class or asking your principal to read to your students. Principals need to feel valued, too. In addition, principals love spirit-wear so provide him or her with a school shirt of the sport or activity you sponsor or personally invite him or her to a game.
Don't Be Shy About Celebrating with Your Principal	Keep your principal informed of student and classroom successes. Share positive notes and emails you receive from parents with your principal.

Establish Clear Communication	Many conflicts arise from poor communication. You can take the initiative to ensure clarity in your interactions with your administrator. This involves: • Respond promptly to emails • Use clear and concise language in emails and meetings • Document requests and responses to create a record of discussions • Schedule one-on-one meetings to address concerns directly and respectfully Don't be afraid to have a critical conversation-be clear on what you want her to know and what you want her to do for you. In addition, get clarity on what your administrator wants you to know and her expectations of you.
Show Appreciation	Acknowledge your principal's leadership and efforts when earned. Express gratitude in person, in emails or the old-fashioned written note.
Be Intentional with What You Say and How You Say It	These are things that I have heard people say that are relationship crushers; you should avoid saying any of these things to your principal and your principal should avoid saying these things to you: I'm/You're just a teacher! What do you expect me to do about it? That's not how I would do it. We've always done it this way. Just figure it out on your own.
	This isn't a big deal. Just handle it. All you care about is test scores. Why can't you be more like (another teacher or the previous principal)? The anonymous survey or letter said... My hands are tied. I'm not in control of how you feel. I know you're new and don't trust me. I don't trust you either. It's not personal. It's just business. I hold true that the relationship between a teacher and an administrator is critical in creating a positive school culture, and the relationship is both professional and personal. It is very easy to derail a relationship when one party perceives the other to be disrespectful. One of my favorite quotes was from Gracie the Dragon Queen in the series "Bad Monkey": "You Americans love to say it's not personal, it's just business, but know that disrespect is always personal!"

Build Collaborative Relationships with Colleagues	A strong team of supportive colleagues can help support building a relationship with your administrator. You should collaborate with peers to share resources, exchange strategies, and create a network of mutual support. This collective effort not only benefits students but also strengthens your resilience. You should leverage your authority by participating in teacher-led committees or even forming a staff morale committee. Help other teachers work through the admin and work to avoid a mob mentality when there is an issue. Volunteer to mentor a new teacher. Your principal will value your positive influence on our colleagues and your school.
Focus on Solutions, Not Problems	When presenting concerns to your administrator, framing the conversation with potential solutions demonstrates initiative and problem-solving skills. For instance, instead of complaining about a lack of resources, you could propose cost-effective strategies to meet classroom needs. This proactive approach may encourage a more cooperative response from your administrator. If you bring a problem or concern, try to bring at least one resolution.
Leverage Feedback and Self-Reflection	If you struggle to receive constructive feedback from your administrator, seeking input from a trusted colleague or mentor can help you grow professionally and support you emotionally. Self-reflection is also essential; you should regularly assess your own practices and identify opportunities that are most important for you to grow or spend your time on.
Engage with External Support Systems	Professional organizations, teacher unions, and peer networks can provide guidance, resources, and advocacy. These groups can help you navigate difficult workplace dynamics and, if necessary, escalate concerns through appropriate channels.
Advocate for Change Diplomatically	If there is a policy or process within the school that is causing you frustration, bring it to your administrator. Make sure you are prepared to share how the policy or procedure is not beneficial to the students, teachers, or the operation of the school. You are not looking for an immediate solution to the problem, but you can get a gauge on two things: 1. Does your administrator agree there is a problem, and 2. You can get advice on how to proceed.

Coping with challenges when you are not feeling supported can take an emotional toll. If you are struggling to build a positive relationship with your administrator despite utilizing the strategies outlined earlier, it is essential to prioritize self-care. Engaging in stress-management outlets such as journaling, counseling, mindfulness practices, or hobbies outside of work can help maintain emotional well-being. Building a strong support network among friends, family, and trusted colleagues can also provide a sense of balance and perspective. If none of these strategies are effective and the relationship with your principal is severely impacting your joy, consider using your experiences to clearly articulate the type of support you need when interviewing for your next school. Remember, there is always another administrator ready to welcome you with open arms and value your contributions!

Essential Learning Points

1. "Managing up" is critical in building a positive relationship with your principal and protecting your emotional well-being and joy.

2. "Managing up" requires you to clearly articulate and communicate the support you need.

3. There are three parts to "Managing up":
    o First, your principal's inability to show your support may be due to a factor outside his/her control,

    o Second, you should reflect on the level of authority you have as a teacher and focus on the things within your control and

    o Third, you should use appropriate strategies to build a positive relationship with your principal that can protect your emotional well-being and your path to joy.

4. No matter the level of support you receive from your principal or don't receive, you are never stuck. There is always something you can do!

Testimony

I had the privilege of opening a new high school and being selected to serve as the first English Department Chair. I knew my principal from my previous school, and he valued the support and leadership of his department chairs. I was excited to help him build a positive school culture where the teachers had a positive partnership with the administration. I had the respect and trust from my principal to seek the needs of my teachers and I knew he was there to provide support and guidance as needed.

While my teachers came from different schools and had diverse backgrounds and experiences, my goal was to celebrate their individuality but bring them together as one faculty. After surveying my teachers, one consistent commodity that the teachers needed and wanted was MORE TIME: time for collaboration with colleagues, time to plan, and time to take care of the heavy workload on their plates. My department put together committees made up of teachers, parents, and students with the purpose of researching best practices that can build more time into a school schedule. This collaborative effort ended up with a recommendation to adjust the school's bell schedule so that every other Wednesday, the school would begin school two hours late. The benefits of late start Wednesdays were:

- *Teachers had time to spend problem-solving the intricacies of teaching and learning,*

- *Teachers had time to target areas of need and/or improvement and work together to generate strategies and approaches to improve student learning and/or outcomes,*

- *Teachers could focus more on improving teaching and learning to benefit student outcomes and*

- *Teachers had more discretion to use the time for providing students remediation, holding club meetings, or taking care of personal business.*

The recommendation from the teachers was appreciated by our principal and the new schedule was approved. The process made our teachers feel they had a voice in the school, and they were empowered to own the time they gained from the schedule.

In this case, the partnership between the teachers and the administration was necessary to protect something very important to all my teachers: TIME. As a lead teacher, it is critical for me to have a trusting relationship with my teachers and my principal. Because of our trusting partnership with our principal, we were able to build a positive school culture and a school where teachers and students were thriving.

- Kim Premoli, 22 years of experience as a High School Teacher/Administrator

ACTIVITY 8

ACTIVITY 8A: Describe a situation when your principal delivered the support you needed when you needed assistance or were new to school.

_____

_____

_____

_____

_____

ACTIVITY 8B: Describe a policy or process you would change and why.

_____

_____

_____

_____

_____

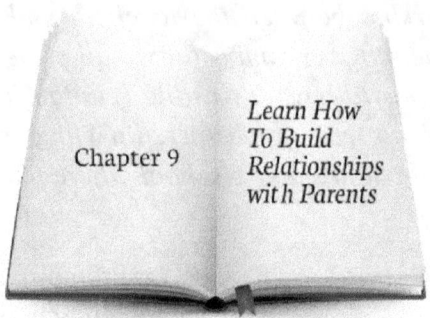

Chapter 9

Learn How To Build Relationships with Parents

"I learned, as a parent, that the more positive my relationship was with my child's teacher and school staff, the more positive the school experience was for my child. It really is that simple but quite impactful."

– Edward J. Spurka

I decided to include a chapter on parents not just because they are a leading source of frustration for teachers but because research shows that when teachers take a proactive and positive approach to building relationships with their students' parents, their job becomes more fulfilling, student performance improves, and the overall school culture thrives.

There is little doubt about the impact parents can have on teacher morale, but questions remain about how much control teachers have over their relationships with parents. I believe that teachers can do more than simply endure difficult parent interactions—they can build trusting relationships that benefit both themselves and their students. By being intentional, relational, and strategic in their interactions, teachers can turn parents into valuable allies who support them in their mission to educate children. In this chapter, I will discuss the importance of the teacher-parent relationship, offer recommendations for building positive relationships with parents, and provide safeguards and advice for navigating even the most challenging parental interactions.

Libby Stanford's article, "Does Parent Involvement Really Help Students?" (EdWeek, 2023), reports:

"When parents are involved in their children's education, students show higher academic achievement, school engagement, and motivation. This was according to a 2019 American Psychological Association review of 448 independent studies on parent involvement."

"When parents become involved at school, for example, attending events such as open houses or volunteering in the classroom, they build social networks that can provide useful information, connections to teachers, or strategies for enhancing children's achievement." (Libby Stanford, July 25, 2023)

At a first-grade open house, Mrs. Stewart noticed that Ann had a large container of sharpened pencils on her shelf. She asked if Ann had purchased them pre-sharpened. Ann explained that she had spent two nights sharpening all 500 pencils for her students. Mrs. Stewart, thinking about how quickly her own son would break the tips, took note. The next morning, Ann received an Amazon delivery at the front office—500 pre-sharpened pencils, courtesy of Mrs. Stewart. Ann was thrilled!

Wouldn't teaching be easier if every parent were like Mrs. Stewart? The reality is that parents have a major impact on a teacher's role. They can either serve as partners who help teachers feel valued or become "energy vampires" who drain their enthusiasm. The teacher-parent relationship is an unavoidable part of the job, one that can either help teachers thrive or make them miserable. I have countless examples of parents behaving badly, and if I compiled them all into a book, I would title it "You Can't Make This Stuff Up." Here are just a few examples from my experience:

- A parent complained to the media because she was not included in selecting the mascot and school colors for a new school I was opening.

- One parent emailed me, threatening to involve Oprah Winfrey if I didn't change her child's English grade.

- A parent blocked my car at a gas station to confront me about her son's math teacher.

- A parent followed me out to my car after work, trying to get their son a parking pass,

- One parent deliberately refused to call me "Dr.," emphasizing "Mr." every time she addressed me, despite my polite correction and

- A parent thought it would be appropriate to land his helicopter on our campus to avoid traffic before his son's soccer match—without giving us any prior notice!

When I met parents for the first time, I always emphasized my belief that their child would be more successful academically and emotionally if we worked together as a team. In my experience, most parents were supportive, like Mrs. Stewart, but the disgruntled and difficult ones—the CAVE people (Citizens Against Virtually Everything)—often demanded the most attention. Over time, I learned that parents could be incredible resources, offering a variety of skills, experiences, and connections that could enhance our school community. For example, when parents asked how they could help, I always found opportunities for them to contribute. Some parents created booster clubs to fund athletic and fine arts programs, while others developed business plans to help raise money for new library furniture. One parent even volunteered to help with the morning carpool for an entire school year. My teachers deeply appreciated parents who showed their support through handwritten notes, snacks, teacher appreciation gifts, and holiday lunches. Because of my intentional efforts to foster strong relationships with parents, they played a vital role in shaping our school's culture. The award I am most proud of in my career is being named Outstanding Principal of the Year—twice—by the State Parent Teacher Association (PTSA).

Navigating relationships with parents is consistently cited as a leading cause of teacher frustration and burnout. In 2017, I surveyed 150 high school teachers, and they ranked "feeling disrespected by parents" as the second most irritating aspect of teaching—right behind workload frustrations. When asked what factors would most improve their daily morale, teachers identified the following:

1. Students saying "thank you."
2. Parents saying "thank you."
3. Effective teamwork
4. Support from colleagues
5. Success of students

Throughout my career, I have worked to build strong relationships with parents by respecting their role and recognizing the challenges they face. Meeting the diverse needs of parents can be overwhelming, but I developed some guiding assumptions that helped me approach these relationships with empathy. I shared these assumptions with my teachers, encouraging them to understand that while we are teaching children, we often find ourselves guiding their parents as well. Many parents are still learning how to parent. It is easy to view parents as adversaries, but doing so makes an already challenging job even harder. Instead, I have found that starting from a place of understanding and meeting parents where they are—not where I think they should be—creates a foundation for positive relationships.

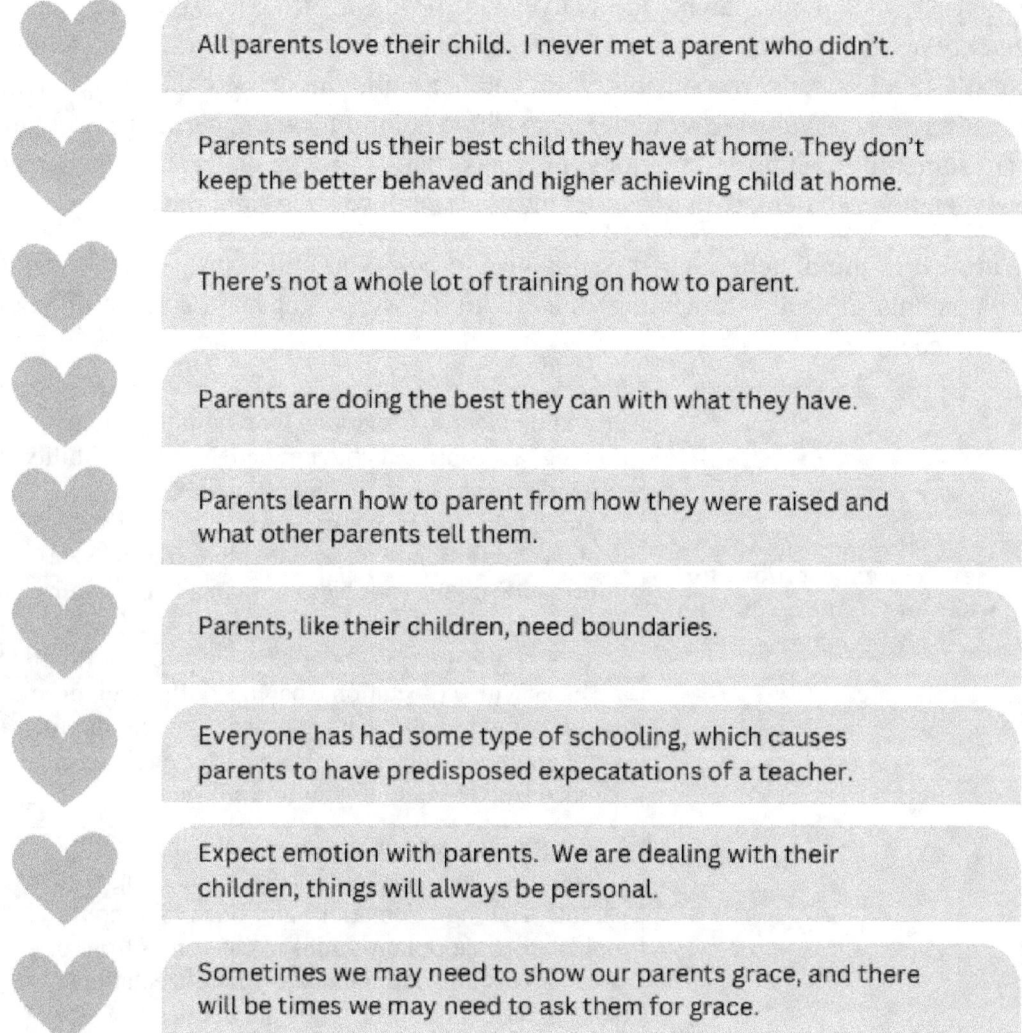

All parents love their child. I never met a parent who didn't.

Parents send us their best child they have at home. They don't keep the better behaved and higher achieving child at home.

There's not a whole lot of training on how to parent.

Parents are doing the best they can with what they have.

Parents learn how to parent from how they were raised and what other parents tell them.

Parents, like their children, need boundaries.

Everyone has had some type of schooling, which causes parents to have predisposed expecatations of a teacher.

Expect emotion with parents. We are dealing with their children, things will always be personal.

Sometimes we may need to show our parents grace, and there will be times we may need to ask them for grace.

One of the biggest surprises for new teachers today is realizing just how emotionally charged interactions with parents can be. Parents, driven by concern for their children, may sometimes express their frustrations in ways that come across as unkind or demanding.

A conversation with my neighbor recently reminded me of what it was like to be a first-year teacher. She had received an email from a parent who was upset that her son had not been invited to a classmate's birthday party. The email's tone caught her off guard, as the parent demanded that she "do something about it." My neighbor was unsure how to respond, so I reassured her that this was likely just an emotional reaction and encouraged her to extend grace.

When she called the parent, the conversation took a different turn. The parent quickly apologized for the tone of the email and admitted that she understood it wasn't the teacher's responsibility to get her child invited to the party. This experience was a valuable reminder that written communication, particularly email, can sometimes amplify emotions in ways that a phone call or face-to-face conversation can defuse. In this case, the phone call was the right move!

With that in mind, here are some strategies to help you build strong relationships with parents while also protecting your emotional well-being and maintaining your joy in teaching.

Set clear expectations for what they can expect from you.	Providing clear expectations for communication, grading, appropriate behavior, and your accessibility will help prevent your parents from getting frustrated. Without clear expectations, you give parents permission to go to each other for information about your class. I've had to deal with parents starting up their own GroupMe to share perceived information about a teacher's class. If you are clear with expectations, parents will spend more time talking about how great you are or complaining about another teacher. Set the expectation that your parents need to come to you for information.
Being accessible demonstrates you are available to their students.	You must let your parents know what their child should do if they need extra help; same thing with parents. Having orientations and Back to School nights are great opportunities to get you in front of your parents and communicate your expectations early in the school year. They are not designated parent conferences, just a chance for you to let parents know your expectations for their students and them. Letting parents know how to contact you and responding to parent emails within 24 hours is important. And make sure you do so, parents sometimes are quick to email your principal. I also recommend that if a parent sends an email that is longer than 3 sentences, pick up the phone and call them. It's better than going back and forth on email. Be careful giving a parent your personal cell number or email. If they do have it, be prepared to set ground rules if they abuse it.

Be visible to parents.	Coach a sport or sponsor a club to show you are invested in your students outside your classroom. Spend time watching your students play sports or perform in the play. Your parents and students will appreciate you being there.
Don't hesitate to have your parents serve in roles that support you and your school.	Having parents serve as Room Moms or Dads or having a parent help you organize volunteers for your class will make your life much easier. A trusted parent can be very helpful in relaying information to other parents like volunteer sign-ups for field days or guest readers. Remember, volunteers are not employees and having a trusted parent help manage them would be very helpful. If you get approval, parents can also help with carpool and lunch duty to help offset your teaching duties.
Include parents in student celebrations.	Inviting parents for student award ceremonies and things like athletic banquets are important to parents. Kindergarten, 6th-grade promotion to middle school, 8th-grade promotion to high school, and, of course, high school graduation are big opportunities to celebrate children. In addition, they are key opportunities to read the names of students and recognize them in front of their parents. It may only take three seconds to read a child's name, but you will create life-long memories for the parents. Most schools give out awards for top academic and athletic achievements. Having a VIP breakfast and having teachers select a student who exhibits positive behavior allows you to recognize more students who are positive role models for your class and school.
Allow parents to engage in school activities and parties.	Book fairs, holiday decorating, and things like Career Day are just a few examples of opportunities to invite parents in to participate in the exciting things at school.
Establish clear and consistent communication.	It is important at the beginning of the school year to let your parents know how you will communicate with them and how they should communicate with you. Communicating academic progress is critical. If your school uses a standard report card that communicates academic progress, it is a good idea to write a narrative to the parents to show their child is known and loved. It personalizes the report card and

	helps educate the parents on their child's academic performance and their child's effort in your class. Weekly classroom notes or newsletters are proactive ways to keep your parents informed. I recommend responding to parent emails within 24 hours unless it is an emergency.
Email etiquette is important.	Here are some things I have advised about email: • After three times back and forth on an email with a parent, pick up the phone and call. • If a parent emails you and you have to research to figure out how to respond to their concern, acknowledge receipt of the email and let the parents know you will get back to them. Don't wait to respond to the parent's email, especially if it might take a few days to get the answer to their question. • When responding to an emotional email from a parent that upsets you, after you write the response, have someone read it over prior to responding, OR step away for five minutes and re-read your response. Sometimes, we can respond emotionally to emotional emails. • Avoid ALL CAPS or multiple exclamation points in your emails!!!
	Triple check sensitive emails to ensure you are sending the email to the correct recipient. I had to once handle a tough situation where a teacher complained about a parent on email. The teacher thought he was sending it home to his wife, but it went to the parent. Oops! Unless it's an emergency, try not to call or email parents on the weekend. You want to be careful not to set the expectation that you are available to them on weekends and on holidays.

There are rules for parent/teacher conferences.	Here are some tips to have a successful parent/teacher conference: It's impossible to be over-prepared for a conference. Set a time limit for the parent conference. If you are worried about a parent conference going too long, schedule the conference 30 minutes prior to school dismissal. Start the parent conference with three things: The purpose of the meeting What do the parents want you to know? What do the parents want you to do? Always stay calm no matter what. Take notes or have someone take notes during the meeting. Email the parent notes of the meeting to provide clarity and make sure you're both on the same page. Always try to start a meeting with something positive about their child, no matter what. Don't talk with parents about other students and their grades. Be careful interjecting while a parent is talking, it's better to let them finish. When it's your time to talk, and they try to interrupt you, you can simply remind them that you didn't interrupt them.
	Don't be afraid to have their child in the meeting, especially secondary students. Be mindful of who should be in the meeting. If the parents surprise you and bring an attorney or advocate to your conference, before proceeding to meet, seek advice from your administrator. I would strongly advise not meeting with more than one family at a time. Sometimes, parents feel more comfortable having other parents in the meeting, especially if their concern involves more than one student. It may take longer, but I would recommend meeting with one family at a time. Remember, you should only discuss the parent's student in the meeting and no other student because of confidentiality.
Maintain your professionalism.	Here are some basic tips that I have found helpful: Provide positive feedback about their child as much as possible. This builds a good foundation of trust and softens the blow if you have to call about their child's inappropriate behavior or poor grade. For every one thing you tell a parent you can't do, give them something they can do. Example: I can't change the grade on the assessment, but if you bring him in before school, we can provide your child with extra help and retest him. Keep all documentation.

	No matter how trivial, you never know when you'll need it.

As a teacher, you have the right to expect professional treatment. Set clear boundaries by posting office hours, and remember that you are not obligated to meet with parents outside of normal school hours. Additionally, unless you have explicitly given permission, parents should address you with the appropriate title—whether it's your last name or "Doctor" (Dr.) if you hold a doctorate degree. How you introduce yourself will let the parent know how to address you. Maintaining this level of respect reinforces your role as a professional.

If a parent ever uses profanity in their communication with you or makes you feel intimidated, notify your administration immediately for support. Disrespectful or inappropriate behavior from parents should never be tolerated. In cases where a parent becomes abusive, request assistance from an administrator to facilitate communication, including parent conferences.

I hope these tips empower you and give you greater confidence when interacting with parents.

While parents can be an incredible resource if given the right opportunities to contribute, it's also important to establish boundaries regarding what they should and should not be able to do. If any parent or group of parents becomes a source of frustration, don't hesitate to seek support from your supervisor or fellow teachers.

I always reminded my more challenging parents:

"Your child will have the greatest chance for success if we work together and are on the same side."

I hope you consistently find yourself surrounded by parents who are eager to partner with you. Stay positive and let your joy shine in the classroom and in activities that involve parents. Even with more difficult parents, happiness is contagious—you may discover that your ability to educate and influence parents is just as impactful as your ability to educate their children.

Essential Learning Points

1. If you are proactive and strategic in building relationships with your students' parents, you will find they can be amazing resources to you and help you focus on what you were called to do: teach children.

2. It is important to set clear expectations for your parents from the beginning of the school year.

3. It is important for you to share with your parents what they can expect from you, including how you will communicate, how their child will be assessed, and how their child can get extra help if he or she needs it.

4. It is appropriate to expect to be treated as a professional, and in some cases, you may have to establish boundaries with some parents.

5. Just like your students, you should meet your parents where they are and not where you think they should be.

6. There are many strategies you can incorporate to be proactive in building a relationship with your parents and, at the same time, protect your emotional well-being and joy.

Testimony

One of the highlights of my career was being selected to open my district's new high school and serve as the school's first football coach. I was blessed to have a year to plan to hire my assistant coaches and prepare for our school's first football game. After serving as an assistant coach for many years, I had the knowledge and experience to build a program from the ground up.

Opening a new school was very exciting as I got to see the construction of our stadium, and I was involved in the ordering of all our equipment and uniforms. I left an established program that had all the bells and whistles and realized that I would have significant challenges providing my players with the same experience in the new program because of limited funding and coaches.

I had always believed in the importance of building positive relationships with my parents and knew I needed their help. My new parents were excited and motivated

117

to help with our new football program, and I was able to organize a strong volunteer parent group called a booster club. The goal of our booster club was to build excitement for our program by raising money and providing a world-class experience for our students. Because of my parents, we were able to raise money for tackling dummies, helmets, and uniforms. More importantly, the program benefitted from the time and energy my parents spent building they spent building with me, my coaching staff, and my school community. In my first year, several parents ended up joining my staff and helped build our feeder program.

It was an honor being selected to start the program, but there is no way I could have done it without my parents.

– Coach Craig Bennett, 28 years of experience teaching History and serving as head football coach

ACTIVITY 9

ACTIVITY 9.1: List 3 things you can do to create a stronger partnership with your parents.

_____

_____

_____

_____

_____

ACTIVITY 9.2: The first time you meet with your parents at orientation, before school starts, how do you introduce yourself and your expectations?

_____

_____

_____

_____

_____

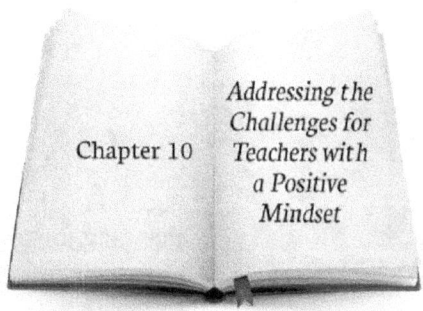

Chapter 10   *Addressing the Challenges for Teachers with a Positive Mindset*

"Keep your thoughts positive because your thoughts become your words,

Keep your words positive because your words become your behavior,

Keep your behavior positive because your behavior becomes your habits,

Keep your habits positive because your habits become your values,

Keep your values positive because your values become your destiny."

– Mahatma Gandhi

Liz is 47 years old and has been teaching for 25 years. She began her career in primary school but has spent the past 20 years teaching math at the secondary level. After a particularly challenging year following COVID, Liz confided in her husband that she wasn't sure she could make it another five years until she was eligible for retirement. She started questioning whether her current salary was worth the increasing challenges she faced—working with three new teachers in her math department, adjusting to the third principal in six years, and managing a growing number of students with behavioral issues.

Recently, a friend approached Liz with an opportunity to work for a private online tutoring program, where she had the potential to earn more money than she was making in the classroom. One of the most appealing aspects of the job was the ability to work from home. Intrigued by the possibility of a career change, Liz decided to weigh her options carefully. She made a list of the positives and negatives of leaving her teaching career after 25 years to take on a tutoring position.

PROS of Leaving Teaching	CONS of Leaving Teaching
Better work-life balance	Been in a school for 25 years, and changing jobs was scary.
Could still work with students by tutoring	Would be leaving the friends she had at her school
Working from home would save money on gas and wear and tear on the car	If she worked five more years, she would be eligible to draw a pension on her retirement plan
Could earn more money at the tutoring company	In five more years, she would get a cheaper rate on her and her husband's health insurance. If she left now, she would have to figure out the benefits.
	The tutoring company would be ideal if she did it after she retired in five years.

Liz's situation is not unlike the one that thousands of teachers face year after year. The question many educators ask themselves is, "Is it worth sacrificing my emotional well-being and my joy to keep teaching?" The increasing workload, ongoing changes in her job, and stagnant salary all contributed to Liz contemplating leaving the classroom.

After carefully weighing the pros and cons of such a significant decision, Liz decided to stay for five more years. Her retirement plan provided long-term financial stability, and the health benefits were crucial for both her and her husband. This reflection helped her recognize the value of continuing her teaching career, but it also made her realize that if she was going to commit to five more years, some changes were necessary. She was determined to reclaim her positivity and become the best teacher she could be—but more importantly, the best wife and mother. Liz acknowledged that while there were many aspects of her job she couldn't change, she had the power to adjust certain things in both her professional and personal life to bring more joy and fulfillment. The first step in this journey was crafting her own Personal Vision Statement:

In order to sustain my emotional well-being and cultivate more joy, I am committed to:

- Being the best wife and mother by having dinner each night with my family.

- Focusing on a better work-life balance by not doing schoolwork on weekends.

- Finding an activity to enjoy with my husband.

- Becoming more involved in my church.

- Engaging my family in a service project.

- Exploring coaching or sponsoring a school activity.

- Taking an art class to nurture my personal interests and creativity.

I love that Liz took the initiative to identify what truly made her feel fulfilled and took greater ownership of her well-being. She became more intentional about spending quality time with her family and pursuing personal passions, such as her art class. Her family also had the opportunity to travel to South America on a mission trip with their church, an experience that strengthened their bond. Additionally, she and her husband found joy in cooking together each night, turning mealtime into a shared experience. As a result of her renewed mindset and the intentional changes she made, Liz found greater joy and a much-improved work-life balance.

Liz's experience highlights some of the key reasons why teachers leave the profession. She was concerned about salary limitations, the increasing number of students with behavioral challenges, and the high turnover rate among both teachers and administrators at her school. Based on my own experience and research in education, I have compiled a list of the most significant barriers preventing teachers from experiencing joy both in the classroom and in their personal lives.

"There will always be barriers that stand in the way of becoming the best teacher you can be. But with a positive mindset and the understanding that no barrier is insurmountable, it is possible to protect your emotional well-being and your joy."

This last chapter dives deeper into the factors that are having the greatest impact on teacher burnout. Hopefully, this book has provided you with some useful and practical strategies that can help you with your path to joy in the classroom and beyond. My hope is that as you continue to build and sustain your path to joy, you will spread joy to others who may be feeling stuck or burned out.

"Joy is contagious! Cultivating a positive mindset and being intentional about protecting your emotional well-being can have a tremendous impact on your students, colleagues, administrators, and even parents. Never underestimate your influence!"

In this chapter, I will explore the top challenges (Barriers) teachers face and share my perspective on how we can sustain our joy. Each barrier is not only surmountable but can be completely dismantled. My goal is to show that with a positive mindset, emotional well-being, and an unwavering commitment to joy, you can successfully navigate any of these challenges that may come your way.

1. Perception of Teachers

Each year at our opening faculty meeting, I would tell my teachers there is one thing I never want to hear them say: "I am just a teacher." In building my teachers' confidence, I recognized that there could be poor perceptions of teachers and teaching in general outside the school building. What makes our profession different from any other is that every stakeholder, from parents to government officials, has had some amount of schooling; therefore, they have an opinion on the role and function of a teacher. While most people remember the teachers who had the biggest impact on their lives, we often spend more time talking about the teachers we didn't like.

When it comes to the perception of teachers, those making poor decisions are frequently highlighted on the nightly news, and it's not hard to find movies that depict eccentric teachers who place themselves above their students. Some of you might remember Mr. Hand from Fast Times at Ridgemont High. He was one of the most eccentric teachers ever, as he proceeded to rip up Jeff Spicoli's tardy pass on the first day of school. Mr. Hand was more interested in his rules and making life difficult for his students—at least, that's how Spicoli saw it. And do you remember the song "Another Brick in the Wall" by Pink Floyd?

We don't need no education,

We don't need no thought control,

No dark sarcasm in the classroom,

Teachers, leave them kids alone,

Hey! Teachers! Leave them kids alone!

(Pink Floyd, 1979)

I remember being introduced to Pink Floyd by my Uncle Bobby, and when you're 12, lyrics can mean a lot. This song certainly isn't complimentary of teachers. Similarly, the band name Lynyrd Skynyrd was a backhanded tribute to a high school gym teacher notorious for his opposition to long hair.

I recognize that perceptions of teachers have deterred young children and young adults from aspiring to enter the profession. Even when I was growing up in the '80s, the standard answers to "What do you want to be when you grow up?" were doctor, lawyer, or professional athlete. Teachers were respected, but they didn't seem as esteemed as other professions. However, when you see negative stories on the news, remember that there are millions of teachers doing amazing things every day, and those negative portrayals do not define our profession.

I can enjoy movies like Fast Times at Ridgemont High for their humor, but I truly appreciate films that showcase dedicated teachers answering their calling and believing in their work. I prefer watching shows like Welcome Back, Kotter or movies like Dangerous Minds, The Ron Clark Story, Dead Poets Society, and Remember the Titans. As for the news, I recognize the media has a job to do, but I wish they spent more time highlighting the heartwarming stories teachers create every day.

People's perceptions become their reality. Continue to advocate for our profession and surround yourself with others who celebrate the heroes that you are!

2. Compensation

Compensation was the number one reason teachers were leaving the profession, according to McKinsey and Company (2023). Forty-eight percent of educators are planning to leave the field due to compensation, while 42% have already left for the same reason. Only 34% of teachers reported satisfaction with their salaries and benefits.

While research indicates that teachers make less than professionals with similar educational backgrounds, education offers many opportunities to supplement a teacher's salary and increase income. While salaries and benefits vary from nation to nation, the most common way to supplement a teaching salary is by earning an advanced degree. District salary schedules are typically structured based on two factors: years of experience and advanced degrees. I would advise you to research or speak with your supervisor about how obtaining an advanced degree could impact your salary.

Here are some other opportunities to add to your teaching salary:

Many schools offer the opportunity to earn money through stipends: money paid for a specific task outside of teaching, which could include: • Coaching a sport • Sponsoring a club like the Student Council or National Honor Society • Working on a district or school initiative • Helping with school operations like covering detention or overseeing textbooks
Teaching summer school
Attending summer workshops or presenting at a workshop
Tutoring after school or during the summer
Teaching summer school
Driving a bus or helping with other operational duties like supervising athletic games

Most governmental educational systems offer their employees things that can be considered compensation outside of salary. These include things like a health benefit plan that can include dental and vision coverage. In addition, there are several other benefits schools and school districts can provide their teachers.

Pension Contributions
Paid-time off for sick and personal leave
Housing allowances
Life insurance
Disability insurance
Relocation expense coverage
Tuition reimbursement for certification or advanced degree
Tuition discounts for a teacher's child/children

3. Expectations

Earlier in this book, I discussed a leading factor of teacher burnout: teachers feeling overworked and undervalued. Teachers face immense pressure to meet the demands of their jobs while balancing the diverse expectations of students, administrators, and parents. With larger class sizes, lingering pressures from COVID-19, and the expectation to personalize learning for each student, teaching has become more challenging than ever before. Additionally, educators must manage increasing numbers of students with learning differences and those on medication to treat ADHD. The rapid advancement of technology has also added new responsibilities, requiring teachers to respond to emails, update parents on student progress, and keep pace with the impact of artificial intelligence.

Beyond the workload, one of the greatest challenges teachers face is feeling undervalued. Many are made to feel that their efforts are never enough due to ever-changing expectations from administrators and the unrelenting high standards set by parents. This persistent pressure can be disheartening. However, the good news is that with a positive mindset, you have more control than you might think!

1. You are in control of the expectations that matter most

2. You are in control of the expectations, you need clarity.
You have the authority to manage up with your administrator and use your authority with your parents to better understand two things:
> What do you want me to know?
> What do you want me to do?

I wanted to ensure I fully understood what was expected of me—particularly by my supervisors. Before I could determine which expectations I could or could not meet, I needed complete clarity on what those expectations were. I probably drove my supervisors crazy with my questions, but I was adamant about knowing exactly what they expected of me.

Understanding others' expectations of us is crucial, but just as important is setting our own expectations for others when appropriate. To help with this, I've created two tables: (1) the things you have a right to expect as a teacher and (2) the things for which you will need to set expectations for others. One of the biggest sources of stress is a lack of clarity around expectations, so taking the time to define them can make a significant difference.

YOU HAVE THE RIGHT TO EXPECT FROM:

YOUR SUPERVISOR	YOUR PARENTS	YOUR STUDENTS
Your compensation	Respect	Be on time for school/class
Your benefits	Trust	Participation in their learning
Your work hours	Volunteering	Complete classwork and homework
How you will be evaluated		Be respectful and behave appropriately.
School policies/procedures		Abide by the academic expectations you set
School safety plan		Abide by the behavioral expectations. you set
Support with student management		
Support with parents		

YOU HAVE THE RIGHT TO SET EXPECTATIONS WITH:

YOUR SUPERVISOR	YOUR PARENTS	YOUR STUDENTS
The level of support you need with your instruction	How you will communicate their student's progress	Academic expectations, including grading and homework policies
The level of support you expect with student management	How you want your parents to communicate with you	Expectations for behavior in class
The level of support you expect in dealing with parents	When you will respond to emails (if you get one on Friday after 4:00)	Consequences for appropriate and inappropriate behavior
Your expectations for professional development	Volunteer opportunities	Grading weights and percentages
	Your office hours or when you're available	Opportunities for remediation/recovery
		When you are available for extra help

Trust me, if you try to make everyone happy and allow everyone around you to set expectations of you and your work, it will make teaching and life so much harder. Clarity of what you expect from others and what others expect from you helps you focus on the things you can control.

4. Your Well-Being

In the McKinsey and Company survey (2023), teachers reported that concerns for their "well-being" were a leading factor in why they got burned out. Teachers reported that they felt the job was too much and the energy that was drained was impacting their personal lives. The time and energy needed to be successful in the job affected their ability to have a healthy work-life balance. The overall workload of a teacher is enough for 40-plus hours a week!

Here are a few things that you can do that will help you navigate these pressures and be able to embrace these issues as they arise:

Collaboration	Planning lessons with your grade level or subject team gives you fresh ideas and takes some pressure to come up with every activity and assessment. Collaboration also can validate your work and help you feel valued, especially if you're helping your colleagues.
Teamwork	Working in teams or serving on committees can help share the load of operational duties. If your team is charged with bus duty, if you work together, you can come up with a schedule for which days work best for you. Working as a team can help you build relationships and serve as emotional support.
Principal's Advisory Council	If your school doesn't have one, it would be good to recommend one. A principal's advisory council provides you access to leadership so that your principal can understand first-hand the pressures on teachers and the opportunities to help them. A school principal has a lot of authority in leading a school.
Mindset	Focus on making sure your personal life compliments your teaching. Find something that takes your mind off work and focus on our mental health. I still cut my own grass every week because it gives me a sense of accomplishment and pride. Some people escape to a good book or run a couple miles each day.
Chunk Time	One of the benefits of being a teacher is having time off for some of the summer and most holidays. There are breaks built into the school calendar where you can chunk your time and look forward to that three-day weekend at Labor Day weekend. If you are overwhelmed with work, know that you will get a break soon.
Protect Your Time	Check your email at least once a day, but don't respond to emails after work or after 4:00 on Friday and never on the weekends unless it's an emergency. Protect your personal time, and never feel guilty for taking time for yourself.
Find the Right School for You	Find a school that is the best fit for you. Find a school that fits your passion for education based on location, socio-economic status, programs offered, and compensation. There are schools that are traditional, hybrid, on-line, and many other structures

	that provide some choices that can align with your values and personal needs. If you prefer a large traditional high school where you can teach 9th grade Political Science all day and you love Friday night football, there is a school for you.
Money	Instead of constantly using your own money for bulletin boards, class supplies, and stickers for your students, ask to see what funds are available from the school. Ask your principal what funds are available from the parent organization or business partners you may not be aware of. Also, check on what fundraising opportunities might be available.

Just like our students have individual needs, today's administrators need to understand that teachers do, too. You don't need permission to invest in yourself and protect your emotional well-being and your joy. In any job, there are going to be things we don't like to do, maybe it's lunch duty or driving a bus. This is why having a support structure of teacher teams, school committees, and a principal's advisory can lessen the load. If you are feeling out of balance, refer to your personal vision statement and implement some strategies that can instantly refocus you and bring you joy!

5. Leadership

Leadership—and the lack of support from leadership—has been a significant factor in why teachers leave the profession. It was also one of the primary reasons cited by many of the teachers I interviewed for open positions at my school. I remember one teacher saying, "The principal at my school didn't even know my name." This sentiment is reinforced by a McKinsey & Company survey, which found that 30% of teachers interviewed cited leadership as a key contributor to burnout.

When working with your administrator and "managing up," you should expect your administrator to be available and invested in your success—especially if they were the ones who hired you. Don't hesitate to communicate what support you need and what that support looks like for you. As teachers, we have diverse needs, and we cannot expect our principals to be mind readers. Some of us appreciate public recognition for a job well done, while others prefer a private handwritten note. Before concluding that you are not supported, take the time to clearly define what "support" means to you.

It is then essential to communicate two key points to your administrator regarding the support you need to be successful in your role:

1. What do you want them to know?
2. What do you want them to do?

If your principal or leader is unable to provide the support you seek, you should expect an explanation. Is it due to policy constraints? Budget limitations? Or is it simply a matter of differing perspectives? Understanding the reasons behind a lack of support empowers you to manage your response and expectations accordingly. Most school leaders were once teachers themselves, and they should remember what it was like to be in the classroom. They should empathize with you and be transparent about the reasoning behind their decisions.

6. Workplace Flexibility

Workplace flexibility is defined as a teacher's inability to have a voice in their general teaching duties, such as their teaching schedule and curriculum. Additionally, teachers often lack the flexibility to manage personal responsibilities, like attending doctor's appointments, due to the rigid structure of their schedules. With curriculum standards and assessments largely dictated by government agencies and district leaders, teachers may feel frustrated by these constraints. To navigate this challenge, it is important to understand the non-negotiable aspects of the curriculum and the standards that both you and your students are accountable for. However, you still have control over the activities and teaching methods you use to engage your students. Focus your time and energy on what you can control, and remember to provide your students with plenty of opportunities to take ownership of their learning.

The good news is that some schools offer alternative school calendars and flexible approaches to curriculum delivery. Hybrid schools, for example, may provide virtual teaching days where teachers can work from home or pre-record lessons in advance. Educators have options when selecting a school that aligns with their flexibility needs. Recognizing the demand for greater workplace flexibility, some schools have incorporated virtual days or professional development days staggered throughout the year. Others have adopted modified block scheduling, allowing teachers additional planning time on designated days.

Taking a personal or sick day was always difficult for me for many reasons—the time required to prepare sub plans and the anxiety of my students missing a day of instruction from me. After all, I was held accountable for their performance. Teachers often struggle with scheduling essential appointments due to the limited flexibility of a typical school day. I personally found it challenging to see my doctor, as their office did not always offer hours past 4:00 p.m., leaving me with few options for scheduling appointments.

My teachers worked in teams to manage up to me to come up with these strategies to have more work flexibility:

1. Teachers worked together to cover each other's classes by staggering their planning periods.
2. Teachers worked to take care of personal appointments during their planning period in secondary school and during specials in primary school. I approved the recommendation that teachers would not have to use their sick or personal leave for an appointment that was less than two hours off campus. I didn't want teachers to feel bad about taking time off to take care of personal things, and I recognized the number of hours my teachers worked outside school hours.
3. Teachers worked to change the work week where Wednesdays had a two-hour late start. This allowed the teachers to work in collaborative groups, grade papers, and provide remediation to their students. It gave the teachers a valuable resource: time.

As a teacher, we are afforded the perk of having some time over the summer off and time off for spring break and most holidays. I did my best to take care of some personal things during these breaks, like getting my car's oil changed. If you need to use a day during a school day, don't let it cause you stress. Most schools and school districts provide teachers with a set number of sick days and days that could be used for personal leave. Don't ever feel guilty about taking a day off. They're your days!

In addition to the reasons listed above, two other critical issues are heavily impacting teacher morale and causing teachers to burn out: STUDENT MANAGEMENT AND SCHOOL SAFETY.

For me, there are things you can do to successfully navigate these issues and see them as opportunities to make a difference in the lives of your students rather than a Barrier that can prevent you from having joy in teaching.

7. Student Behavior

On July 12, 2022, the NCES released an update to the January 2022 through December 2022 collections of the School Pulse Panel, reporting that 56% of schools believe student behavior has worsened since COVID-19. There has been an increase in classroom disruptions due to student misconduct (56%), rowdiness outside the classroom (49%), and acts of disrespect toward teaching staff (48%).

Today, more parents are focused on their child's self-esteem, and more schools have implemented positive reinforcement strategies as a primary means to maintain appropriate student behavior. However, teachers often feel their hands are tied when handling students who exhibit inappropriate behavior. This not only leads to disengagement from learning but also creates a distraction for the entire class. I want to acknowledge that this is a significant challenge, but I also want to reassure you that you should never feel solely responsible for managing students with persistent behavioral issues. While you are responsible for setting expectations and implementing strategies to reinforce appropriate behavior and correct misconduct, you should not have to handle these challenges alone. Support from administration, colleagues, and school-wide policies should be in place to assist you in creating a positive learning environment.

Here are some things you can do:

1. Ensure your students, no matter what grade level, are clearly aware of your expectations. Share these expectations with the parents as well.

2. Be sure to show your children that you are disappointed in their behavior, not them. For my "why," I believe all children need someone to believe in them. Encourage the heart to reinforce positive behavior as much as possible and confront negative behavior immediately.

3. Document, Document, Document. Document the expectations you have for your class, the inappropriate behavior that has been exhibited, and how you have responded to it. You will need this documentation for number 4.

4. Engage your school's counselor, behavior specialist, and administrator, to observe your class and help provide some strategies to help correct your student's inappropriate behavior.

5. Be in constant contact with the child's parents.

6. Continue to try to connect and build relationships with our students. If your student plays a sport outside of school or works, try to go to a game or visit their place of employment. If you can make just one personal connection, it could be a game-changer for the child. This worked for me with several students.

It would be wonderful if our classes were full of angels who came to class ready to learn, with perfect manners. We all know that the reality is that teachers are expected to be content experts and behavior analysts. The beauty of working in a school is we can start new each year or in the upper grades, each semester. Start firm, and you can always ease up. A new 9th-grade teacher, on the third week of school, decided that she would no longer let her students use profanity in her class. When she announced this, the boys had a fun time asking her to clarify which words were inappropriate, as they listed every profane word they could think of. The problem was the teacher didn't confront their profanity the first few weeks of school and when you don't confront negative behavior, it becomes the norm. Confront everything in the beginning!

Early in this book, I challenged you to think about teachers who had a big impact on you. Think about this: a year from now, your students may not remember the grade in your class or any of your lessons, but they will remember the impact you had on them. You never know the impact you can have on a student, especially the students who demand more of your time and attention. When I was a new high school principal, I missed the classroom and teamed up with one of my English teachers to teach a class called Freshman Focus. Our vision was to connect with the students who were identified as "at-risk" to drop out of high school. We hand-selected our twelve boys and taught them everything from English to social skills. Rafael was 15 when he took our class, and eighteen years later, he's the first person who texted me on my birthday! You can't put a price on that, and each year, he reminds me of my WHY!

8. School Safety

When I was a sophomore in high school, our drama department was putting on the play Once Upon a Mattress. As part of the set, 15 mattresses were stacked on the auditorium stage. My public speaking class was held in a drama classroom adjacent to the auditorium. One day, I smelled smoke coming from the stage, and when I walked behind it, I saw that the mattresses were on fire. I ran down the hall as fast as I could to alert the office. Two of my classmates got into serious trouble for smoking, and I received a letter of appreciation from my superintendent. To this day, I still joke with my wife that I saved our high school! From that moment on, I was serious about fire drills.

In the 1980s, school safety wasn't a major concern. I never worried about my safety, and school shootings weren't something we thought about. That changed in 1999 with the Columbine High School shooting, which altered the landscape for schools across the country. I will never forget being in a classroom that year when my students began questioning whether I could keep them safe. When students don't feel safe, they can't learn. Today, ensuring that students feel secure is one of the greatest responsibilities teachers face.

Throughout my career, I have encountered many challenging situations. I responded to a fire in a science classroom and an intruder who entered my school's campus to confront a student. I also remember the shock and paralysis that gripped both teachers and students on September 11, 2001. The reality is that when teachers don't feel safe, they can't teach, and when students don't feel safe, they can't learn. While tragic events have occurred in schools across the nation, the implementation of improved safety protocols and procedures has made schools more secure.

Open communication between teachers and administrators is critical. When teachers feel supported by their administration, they gain confidence in their school's commitment to both their success and their safety. It is essential to know your responsibilities in an emergency and ensure that your students do as well. If you or your students have any questions, concerns, or suggestions regarding safety plans, you have an obligation to advocate for change by bringing them to your administration. Here are some steps you can take to feel safer at school:

Know your school's internal and external safety plans, including fire, bomb threat, intruder, evacuation, hard and soft lockdown, and reunification.

Ensure that your students understand their roles in these plans and that these plans are practiced.

Constantly build positive relationships with your students and fellow teachers. When you build trusted relationships, people will alert you to things. Practice "See Something, Say Something."

Build collaborative teams with your fellow teachers. If you have a concern, chances are, someone else probably has the same concern.

If you have safety concerns or need assistance with any situation that makes you feel uneasy, don't ever be afraid to ask for help and "manage up."

Make sure there is a clear process for students, teachers, and parents to voice concerns regarding safety. Many schools offer anonymous tip lines in addition to direct communication with the administration.

I have listed the most common factors that are contributing to teachers leaving the profession or burning out. I hope that I demonstrated that with a positive mindset and being intentional in protecting your emotional well-being, you will be able to overcome any challenge or barrier that comes your way, as I did. Remember, you won't be able to control everything that comes your way, but you are able to control how you respond. My hope is that you will benefit from the strategies I presented and you will be intentional and persistent in investing in yourself.

With the continuing challenges of artificial intelligence, increasing demands from government officials, school administrators, and parents, and the importance of serving as positive role models for our students, the need for dedicated and passionate teachers like you is more important than ever before.

I know my book is not exhaustive of every challenge facing teachers around the world, but I do believe the strategies presented can be beneficial professionally as well as personally. Teaching is one of the most rewarding yet challenging professions, and you don't have to navigate it alone. If you're looking for additional resources, support, or a community of like-minded educators, visit me at Spurkaedinstitute.com. I'd love to hear your experiences, insights, and success stories as we continue this journey together.

Essential Learning Points

1. A positive mindset and being intentional in protecting your emotional well-being and your joy will help you overcome any barrier you may face.

2. In every situation, remember that you are always in control of more than you think.

3. We all have a barrier or barriers that cause us the most stress. Lean on your personal vision statement and your strategies to protect your emotional well-being and joy. But know this: you don't have to do it alone. There is always someone to support you and someone who went through the same challenge you are going through. Never be afraid to ask for help.

4. Most important, your positive mindset and resilience to protect your joy are stronger than any challenge that can come your way!

ACTIVITY 10

ACTIVITY 10.1: You are at a conference that includes teachers, business leaders, and people from the health field. A non-teacher makes a statement to you, "I don't know how you deal with parents today. I could never do that." As a spokesperson for teachers, how do you respond to this statement? Feel free to use any other barriers that exist for teachers. How would you respond?

_____

_____

_____

ACTIVITY 10.2: You are invited to speak to a class full of seniors to represent teaching as a profession. What is the message you share with the students on the positive aspects of teaching?

_____

_____

_____

FINAL THOUGHTS

I was blessed to have had such a positive school experience growing up, where I felt my teachers knew me and genuinely cared about my success. I believe my friends and I probably gave our teachers just as much trouble as kids do today. However, as challenging as teaching was in the 1980s, educators today face even greater difficulties. They didn't have to deal with parent emails, cell phones, or social media. The news didn't scrutinize educators daily, and school shootings were unheard of. Back then, if I misbehaved at school, I was more worried about what my parents would do than any consequences from the school itself. I never got into trouble, but my friends Jeff and Eric did. I remember seeing them in the principal's office during our Homecoming Dance. Their fathers didn't care about giving them due process, and my parents were no different. There seemed to be a greater respect for teachers and administrators in those days.

Looking back over my 33-year career, I often wonder how I was able to remain resilient and maintain my love for education for so long. I am incredibly grateful for my career and have so much to celebrate. I have been honored by the Governor, the State PTSA, and my local school system. I was even named Citizen of the Year by the Milton Police Department. However, the achievement I am most proud of is the relationships I built with hundreds of teachers and thousands of students. It makes my day when I walk into an Urgent Care with a hat on and unshaven, and the nurse still recognizes me, saying, "Hello, Dr. Spurka!" It warms my heart to know that my students remember me.

As wonderful as my career was, it wasn't without its challenges. There were moments when my passion for education was shaken and times when I seriously questioned whether it was time to walk away. When I first moved to Georgia, a teacher told me I should go back up north and called me a "damn Yankee." According to them, a "damn Yankee" was someone who moved south and never left. I've been turned down for jobs and promotions because I wasn't considered a good fit. I've had leaders who believed in me and invested in my success, and I've had others who were more focused on test scores or simply didn't have time for me.

One of the most difficult moments in my career came when I was evaluated based on an anonymous parent survey. Out of 300 comments, six individuals left 26 negative remarks about my leadership. My supervisor took only those negative comments, inputted them in ChatGPT, and used the generated summary as my evaluation. Despite the fact that 274 comments were positive, they were completely disregarded. That was a true test of my resilience.

My wife constantly reminds me that feedback is a gift, but to this day, I cringe at the thought of anonymous surveys. My confidence was shaken many times, yet I managed to persevere. Today, I can look back on my career with immense pride and joy.

As a child and young adult, I just wanted to be liked and respected. Now, I understand that it's impossible to be appreciated by everyone. I've learned that if I let everything people say about me get under my skin or if I try to be everything to everyone, I will only end up miserable and pleasing no one. The most important lesson I've learned is to be true to myself and stay connected to my purpose in life. Teaching was never just a job for me—it was my calling. Even on the hardest days, I never doubted that I was blessed to be an educator.

If there's one thing I hope you take away from this book, it's this: As challenging as teaching can be, it is one of the most rewarding ways to impact a child's life outside of parenting. Every word and action, no matter how small, has the potential to shape a student's future. I am constantly amazed by how many former students I run into who remember me—and how many I remember. Even the students who drove me crazy and spent countless hours in my office still come back to check on me. I know that educators don't always feel valued or appreciated, but trust me, the true reward of teaching is the impact you have on the lives of your students.

Whether you teach pre-K, elementary, middle, or high school, you play a vital role in each student's journey. When they walk across the stage at graduation, you share in that moment. Thank you for helping to shape the next generation of teachers, doctors, lawyers, military personnel, and professionals in every field. Your work is invaluable.

Believe in yourself, invest in yourself, and most importantly, be joyful, my friend!

Tribute to my Teachers:

Thank you for helping me grow into the person I am today:

Mom and Dad, who were my first teachers who taught me to have good manners and be kind to others,

Pop-Pop and Mom-Mom who encouraged me to do my best in sports and not worry about winning or losing,

Grandpop, who talked about the Phillies whenever I saw him,

My Uncle Bobby, who introduced me to Gene, Paul, Peter, and Ace (KISS),

Mrs. Schaffer, for opening the door on my first day of school,

Mrs. Ely, who let us celebrate the Phillies' World Series championship in 1980,

Mr. Duvall, who called my mom into school to let her know I had some smarts,

Mr. Meyers, who gave me detention after I called him Arnie,

Coach Wagner and Coach Lutner, who picked me up at my house and crammed us into your car for basketball games (I loved Coach Lutner's Dukes of Hazzard car),

Mr. Buckly, Rich's dad, who picked us up in his Volkswagon Beatle bus to go to baseball games,

Joe Marshall, who was my favorite Santa Claus but not my favorite umpire (he struck me out when the ball hit the plate),

Mr. Hengel, who tied Jeff's arm to his body so he could learn how to shoot a basketball,

Mr. Testa and Mr. Wagner who competed to see which coach could hit the baseball onto the roof of the junior high school,

Mr. Burkhardt who taught me, "If you want to go fast, go slow."

Mrs. Maggioncalda told me, "I don't know," when I asked if your pubic hair turns gray when you get old (this was during sex ed class),

Mr. Ollie, who made me laugh when his dress shirt was sticking out of his zipper, thanks for noticing Eric,

Mr. Watson, who wore a turtleneck every day, including the student/teacher basketball game,

Mr. Warner, who made us chuckle watching the series Shogun when he kept using the word seamen,

Mr. and Mrs. Newton, who checked with Mr. Stetson about this kid, Eddie Spurka, and let him date their daughter, Mr. Newton, thank you for writing us a pass when we snuck out of school to go to lunch,

Coach Pidcock, who believed in me and let me hang out in the gym my entire senior year,

Coach Lorrain (Hank) Ledden, who let me know it was ok to drink a cold Pepsi at halftime when the weather was below 30 degrees,

Coach Stetson, who taught me dedication by driving me to Philly to my grandparents on New Year's Eve so I didn't miss practice,

Coach Chiaro, who would spit his chewing tobacco on the ground next to me while I was stretching in 100-degree temperatures on the football field next to the cow pasture,

Mrs. Gray, who I brought out my love for Algebra and had me sub for her when I was in college,

Mr. Brown, who was one of the best teachers and the reason I took French in college,

Dr. Croddy, who taught me, "if the spinster is tall, then the spinster is tall, is necessarily true,"

Dr. Dayton, who was my advisor who supported me in finishing my dissertation,

Mr. Bob Lynch, who had my back when I was a young administrator and

Dr. Harden and Dr. Stiles how instilled in me to be the best version of myself as an educational leader.

I will always be fond of the things my teachers and coaches did for me, but when it's all said and done, what I will cherish the most is that they made me feel loved!

MEET THE AUTHOR

 Dr. Edward Spurka's distinguished journey in education began with an unexpected detour from his path to law school. What started as a temporary position working with adjudicated youth at The Glen Mills Schools in Pennsylvania ignited a lifelong passion for transforming students' lives, leading him to pursue multiple degrees in education—starting with Special Education from West Chester University in 1992, followed by master's, specialist, and doctorate degrees from the University of Georgia.

Over three decades, Dr. Spurka ascended through every level of education, from counselor and teacher to assistant principal and Head of School. His exceptional leadership garnered four Governor's High-Performance Principal awards and two Outstanding Principal of the Year honors from the Georgia PTA. When selected to establish Cambridge High School from the ground up, he demonstrated his ability to build not just institutions but thriving educational communities.

Shaped by his mentor, Principal Ron Tesch, Dr. Spurka developed a leadership philosophy centered on creating environments where teachers could flourish and students excel. This approach consistently yielded high teacher retention rates and exceptional staff morale across both public and private institutions. "I prided myself in creating school environments where teachers felt valued and supported because they had the biggest impact on my students," he reflects. This unwavering dedication to holistic education and teacher empowerment has cemented his legacy as a transformative figure in education.

Connect with Dr. Spurka at www.SpurkaEdInstitute.com.

References

- Birkman, R. (1995). True Colors/get to know yourself and others better with the highly acclaimed Birkman Method. Thomas Nelson Publishers.
- Bonino, S. (May 3, 2011). Just a teacher. Retrieved from http://beingteacherishblogspot.com.
- Brookhart, S and Guskey, T. (2019). What we know about grading, what works, what doesn't, and what's next. ASCD.
- Cataldi, A. (2023). Loud. Triumph Books.
- Covey, S. (1989). 7 Habits of highly successful people. Blackstone Publishing, Inc.
- Dweck, C. (2007). Mindset, the new psychology of success. How we can learn to fulfill our potential. Ballantine Books.
- Duckworth, A. (2016). Grit: The power of passion and perseverance. Scribner.
- Education Week. Teachers are not ok, even though we need them to be by Madeline Will, September 14, 2021.
- Fine, A. (2010). You already know how to be great. Penguin Group.
- Fink, S B, and Capparell, S. (2013). The Birkman Method, your personality at work. Jossey-Bass.
- Gallup, Inc. (2022). State of the global workplace: 2022 report. Gallup.
- Gordon, J. (2007). The Energy Bus. John Wiley & Sons.
- Greenberg, M. The Stress-Proof Brain. (2017). New Harbinger Publications.
- HuffPost. (2015). How to Stop Worrying. (Cliff Hsia) Retrieved from www.huffpost.com.
- Johnson, S. (1999). Who moved my cheese? Vermilion.
- Kubicek, J and Cochram, S. (2016). Five Voices, how to communicate effectively with everyone you lead. Wiley.
- Mali, T. (2013). What Teachers Make, in praise of the greatest job in the world. Berkley Books, New York.
- McDonald and Hutcheson. (2017) Don't Waste Your Talent: The 8 Critical Steps To Discovering What You Do Best—the Highlands Company.
- McKinsey and Company. (2023). K-12 teachers are quitting. What would make them stay? Retrieved from www.mckinsey.com
- My Forsyth Magazine. The Little Things Make You Feel BIG. (Edward J. Spurka, March 2020).
- National Center for Education Statistics. (2022). School Pulse Panel. Retrieved from www.nces.ed.gov.
- National Center for Education Statistics. (2023). Teacher attrition and mobility report. Retrieved from https://nces.ed.gov.
- National Education Association (NEA). (2022). Retrieved from www.nea.org.
- NITI Aayog report in 2023. Retrieved from www.NITI.Aayog.gov.
- Professional Association of Georgia Educators (PAGE). (2024). Workforce Survey. Retrieved from www.pageinc.org.
- Quenk, N. (2009). Essentials, Myers-Briggs Type Indicator Assessment. Wiley.
- Rath, T. and Clifton, D. (2007). How full is your bucket? Gallup Press.

- Shetty, J. (2020). Think like a monk. Harper Collins Publ. The UK.
- Sinek, S. (2017). Leaders eat last. Penguin.
- Sinek, S. (2009). Start with why: How great leaders inspire everyone to take action. Portfolio/Penguin.
- Stanford, L. (2023). Does parent involvement really help students? Retrieved from www.edweek.org.
- Stiles, D. (2015). Turning Points Coaching and Consulting.
- UK Department of Education (DfE) reported data. Retrieved from www.Gov.UK.
- UNESCO. (2024). Global report on teachers. Paris: United Nations Educational, Scientific, and Cultural Organization.
- The Wall Street Journal. (2022). Report on the 2022 poll by the National Education Association. Retrieved from www.wsj.com.